Inna Mikhaylova

System design for autonomous open-ended acquisition of new behaviors

Inna Mikhaylova

System design for autonomous open-ended acquisition of new behaviors

Bootstrapping of robot's developement

Südwestdeutscher Verlag für Hochschulschriften

Impressum/Imprint (nur für Deutschland/ only for Germany)
Bibliografische Information der Deutschen Nationalbibliothek: Die Deutsche Nationalbibliothek verzeichnet diese Publikation in der Deutschen Nationalbibliografie; detaillierte bibliografische Daten sind im Internet über http://dnb.d-nb.de abrufbar.

Alle in diesem Buch genannten Marken und Produktnamen unterliegen warenzeichen-, marken- oder patentrechtlichem Schutz bzw. sind Warenzeichen oder eingetragene Warenzeichen der jeweiligen Inhaber. Die Wiedergabe von Marken, Produktnamen, Gebrauchsnamen, Handelsnamen, Warenbezeichnungen u.s.w. in diesem Werk berechtigt auch ohne besondere Kennzeichnung nicht zu der Annahme, dass solche Namen im Sinne der Warenzeichen- und Markenschutzgesetzgebung als frei zu betrachten wären und daher von jedermann benutzt werden dürften.

Verlag: Südwestdeutscher Verlag für Hochschulschriften Aktiengesellschaft & Co. KG
Dudweiler Landstr. 99, 66123 Saarbrücken, Deutschland
Telefon +49 681 37 20 271-1, Telefax +49 681 37 20 271-0
Email: info@svh-verlag.de
Zugl.: Bielefeld, Universität, Diss., 2009

Herstellung in Deutschland:
Schaltungsdienst Lange o.H.G., Berlin
Books on Demand GmbH, Norderstedt
Reha GmbH, Saarbrücken
Amazon Distribution GmbH, Leipzig
ISBN: 978-3-8381-1508-5

Imprint (only for USA, GB)
Bibliographic information published by the Deutsche Nationalbibliothek: The Deutsche Nationalbibliothek lists this publication in the Deutsche Nationalbibliografie; detailed bibliographic data are available in the Internet at http://dnb.d-nb.de.

Any brand names and product names mentioned in this book are subject to trademark, brand or patent protection and are trademarks or registered trademarks of their respective holders. The use of brand names, product names, common names, trade names, product descriptions etc. even without a particular marking in this works is in no way to be construed to mean that such names may be regarded as unrestricted in respect of trademark and brand protection legislation and could thus be used by anyone.

Publisher: Südwestdeutscher Verlag für Hochschulschriften Aktiengesellschaft & Co. KG
Dudweiler Landstr. 99, 66123 Saarbrücken, Germany
Phone +49 681 37 20 271-1, Fax +49 681 37 20 271-0
Email: info@svh-verlag.de

Printed in the U.S.A.
Printed in the U.K. by (see last page)
ISBN: 978-3-8381-1508-5

Copyright © 2010 by the author and Südwestdeutscher Verlag für Hochschulschriften Aktiengesellschaft & Co. KG and licensors
All rights reserved. Saarbrücken 2010

Acknowledgments

First of all I am grateful to Prof. Edgar Körner and Andreas Richter for giving me at HONDA Research Institute a unique opportunity to carry out a future-oriented, fundamental research with the possibility to validate the results on a real robot.

I also want to thank the members of the examination board, Prof. Helge Ritter, Prof. Gerhard Sagerer, Dr. Sven Wachsmuth, and Dr. Stefan Kopp from Bielefeld University for their time and willingness to review this thesis.

The implementations and experiments carried out in this work are largely based on the software and the hardware put into practice by my colleagues. Therefore I would like to thank Mark Dunn, Bram Bolder, Achim Bendig, Michael Gienger, Benjamin Dittes, Marcus Stein, Antonello Ceravola, Sven Rebhan, Julian Eggert, Heiko Wersing, Stefan Kirstein, Martin Heracles, Holger Brandl, Jens Schmüdderich, Martin Heckmann, and Tobias Rodemann. I had a good fortune to meet these excellent team-workers who fill the everyday life of a researcher with humor, patience, and cooperativeness.

I am profoundly grateful to Prof. von Seelen, Herbert Janssen, Frank Joublin and Marc Toussaint for the support and fruitful scientific discussions.

My supervisor Dr. Christian Goerick has chosen the best way to guide my research by showing me the valuable goals and granting the freedom to decide about the means. I am deeply indebted to Christian who offered his time and efforts to support my work in all possible ways. Without his razor-sharp analytic mind I would get lost in the jungles of the details that accompanies the research and I would be devoured by the self-doubts without his encouragement.

Finally, I thank my family for their patience and support.

Contents

1 **Introduction and Goals**   3

2 **State of the Art**   7
   2.1 Robotics 7
       2.1.1 Development driven by Intelligent Adaptive Curiosity 9
       2.1.2 Intrinsically motivated Reinforcement Learning 10
       2.1.3 Declarative learning with Discrete Event Dynamic Systems 12
       2.1.4 Comparison of developmental processes for different architectures 13
   2.2 Psychology 16
       2.2.1 Drives of child's development according to Piaget 16
       2.2.2 Principles of development according to Vygodsky 17
   2.3 Neurobiology 18
       2.3.1 Brain development in ontogeny and phylogeny 18
       2.3.2 Models for organization of learning in the brain 19
   2.4 Summary 21

3 **Design of Developing Systems**   23
   3.1 Design of a value system: specific versus unspecific reward 23
   3.2 Design of innate behaviors: provide favorable interaction 25
   3.3 Design of an abstraction layer: beyond reactivity 26
       3.3.1 Requirements for abstraction layer 26
       3.3.2 Formalization and abstraction types 28
       3.3.3 Development of the abstraction layer 32
   3.4 Summary 35

4 **Incremental Building of Developing Systems**   37
   4.1 Learning in interaction and learning to interact 37
       4.1.1 Bootstrapping system: saliency-driven gaze selection 37
       4.1.2 Object learning and recognition 40
       4.1.3 Extension by unspecific reward system for behavior learning 41
       4.1.4 Experimental results 46
   4.2 Exploration of controllability 48
       4.2.1 System instance: autonomous learning of a request gesture 49
       4.2.2 Segmentation of sensorimotor flow into predictive models with the help of a Gaussian Mixture Model 51
       4.2.3 Experimental results 54
       4.2.4 Conclusions 57
   4.3 Expectation generation: beyond reactivity 57

Contents

        4.3.1   Experimental setup and system architecture 59
        4.3.2   Expectation generation and evaluation 63
        4.3.3   Experimental results 68
        4.3.4   Analysis: distribution of learning and predesign 70
        4.3.5   Conclusions 71
    4.4   Summary 72

5 Summary and Conclusions   **75**

List of Used Symbols   **79**

Bibliography   **81**

1 Introduction and Goals

The humans have a long-lasting dream of understanding intelligence and creating artificial intelligent machines that would reproduce human abilities. Initial attempts aimed mainly at systems that can directly solve a specific task under fixed constraints. This approach targeted primarily such abilities as logical inference and planning. However, tests on robots acting in the real world revealed severe problems and led to a shift of the research focus in Artificial Intelligence in the mid eighties. The scientific community was forced to reconsider the question which abilities contribute to what is judged to be intelligent behavior.

Indeed, robots, which are exposed to a huge variety of situations with a necessity to act in real time, make clear that one of the most amazing ability of the human brain is the ability to ask new questions and to find tractable solutions for novel situations. Such autonomous acquisition of a control which is appropriate for a particular system in a particular environment is the subject of the research in modern branches of Artificial Intelligence: Embodied Cognition and Developmental Robotics.

Both Embodied Cognition and Developmental Robotics take as a central concept the dynamic interaction between the system and its environment. Developmental Robotics adds to the interaction yet another dynamics, that of learning and development. Indeed, at the complexity level of the humanoid robots and its interaction with a human it is impossible to preview and pre-design all necessary behaviors and how they should be controlled in all possible situations. The expected benefits of artificial development are a higher degree of adaptivity to unforeseen situations, no necessity to redesign the system every time the task of the robot changes, and finally breaking through the limits of the complexity of hand-designed behaviors.

The research in Developmental Robotics has made a big progress in the investigation of how a system can learn some isolated abilities (for an overview see [34]). However, the focusing on only one ability often has the following consequences:

- the design of the system is specific for the desired ability only and can not be used in a different learning scenario,

- the assumptions concerning the rest of the system are unrealizable (e.g. assumption that the subsystem gets a perfect, grounded teaching signal from the rest of the system),

- the acquired ability is difficult to integrate with other abilities, and

- the learning stops as soon as the desired ability is acquired.

The focus of this work is the design of the development of the system as a whole instead of the design of the learning in an isolated sub-system. Two points are particularly important for our approach: we aim at the autonomous system and task-unspecific, open-ended development. Let us clarify these two points:

1 Introduction and Goals

Autonomous system. True autonomy requires the ability of the system to evaluate the situation according to its own value metric. This evaluation can be implicit (in terms of triggered reaction) or explicit (in terms of activation of an association to expected value). Important is that this evaluation assures the survival (self-maintenance) of the creatures. In the case of robots survival means that the robot does not destroy itself and the designer does not terminate the acting robot because of ill-behaving.

We aim at robots having a complex behavior in a complex dynamic environment. For such settings it is impossible for the designer to preview all the situations and pre-design the appropriate detailed evaluations. The attempts to do so lead to the well-known problems of the GOFAI (Good-Old-Fashioned-Artificial-Intelligence): "symbol grounding problem" and "frame-reference problem" [45]. In our work we ask how to design a core general evaluation and the mechanisms to refine this core evaluation so as to bootstrap the developmental process. Our aim is that the system is complete in the sense that it can autonomously detect and resolve a mismatch between its behavior and survival purposes. We consider core evaluation both in implicit form of innate reflexes and explicit form of innate rewards. In this way the bootstrapping provides the system with the information about both:

- the sort of interaction this particular agent can have in its particular environmental niche, and
- the particular definition of the value metric.

So that we could speak of a situated system in the sense of [45]: *an agent autonomously acquires information from its perspective in the interaction with its environment.*

Task-unspecific, open-ended development. We already mentioned at the beginning of this introduction that the majority of machine learning algorithms use a task-specific learning design. Often the design is very time-consuming and reduces the part to be learned to a very obvious mapping. For example, if the sensor data is first subject to complex preprocessing, it can then happen that the learning design is as time-consuming and as restrictive as a full design of the behavior itself and the system does not really gain in adaptivity and autonomy. Another problem of the narrow task-specific design is that the developmental process stops as soon as the task is learned.

On the other extreme end we have a learning that is not pre-structured at all. The designer's effort is small, but the output is a black-box which does not generalize neither to slightly different situations nor to the slightly different problems. Such black-box learning also introduces a typical problem of distributed representation: the system should care not to destroy the old information while learning the new one. Our intuition is that such unstructured learning can not scale up for a complex task and environment. Therefore our aim is to structure the learning but in a task-unspecific way.

Above we clarified the aim of our work in a descriptive way by explaining our understanding of autonomous, task-unspecific, open-ended development. Below we further clarify our aims in a constructive way by formulating the research questions that we want to answer.

In our work we first ask how to define the system's internal behavior evaluation needed for autonomy in a task-unspecific way. The goal is to have an evaluation that not only allows to solve a specific task in a specific context but also allows the exploration towards new behaviors. We analyze then possible structures that can memorize the evaluation of the system-environment interaction for the purpose of the behavior generation. Based on the formalization of possible memorization structures we investigate how existing abilities create a potential for the development of further abilities. The research objectives listed above reflect our aim at the open-ended task-unspecific development. This thesis is organized as follows. Chapter 2 gives an overview of the research on organization of the development done in robotics, neurobiology and psychology. In Chapter 3 we discuss which general design principles for bootstrapping a developing system can be derived from the biological and psychological insights in order to avoid the problems encountered in current robotics implementations. Chapter 4 validates the proposed design principles on the examples of the implementations. Finally, Chapter 5 summarizes the results and gives an outlook on the possible future research directions.

1 Introduction and Goals

2 State of the Art

The organization of autonomous development is a very general question. Thus there exists a huge amount of related work done in robotics, psychology and neurobiology. The observation of the development in psychology and biology is often reduced to the phenomenological description which does not necessarily help to discover the process that leads to observed phenomena. The same is true for robotics, where the mimicking of the development may reproduce some of the data from experiments with children without being able to generalize to another experiments. However, there exist also considerable amount of work that goes beyond the phenomenological level and aims at understanding the underlying principles. Here we a make a short overview of the ideas that drive the current interdisciplinary research on the organization of development.

2.1 Robotics

Developmental robotics is a young research field. It needs first to formalize used notions and clarify the research aims. By the word "development" the community means autonomous acquisition of skills with progressive increase of the task complexity. This process is also referred to as "ongoing emergence". In order to make this notion more precise [47] formulates the necessary criteria (Table 2.1) to judge whether the robot is developing.

Below we describe major groups of mechanisms that were proposed in Development Robotics for creation of ongoing emergence.

The first group of mechanisms guides development by incremental changes on the morphological level:

- freezing and unfreezing the degrees of freedom of the body control [33],
- change of the mass of muscles and limbs [57], and
- progressively increasing sensor resolution [40].

This approach is largely supported by the findings in psychology and neurobiology. Nevertheless, implementations pursuing the development of the morphology are currently either very simplistic or do not scale in the direction of open-endness. We do not have a possibility to influence directly the robot's morphology. Still we can use the general principle "go from coarse to fine". In order to guide development we can increase incrementally the level of control details (see also discussion in Section 2.3).

The second group of mechanisms proposes to guide the development with the help of a caregiver:

- The caregiver may provide a general support for the learner's interaction with the environment (scaffolding). The caregiver prepares the environment (e.g. for the purpose of

2 State of the Art

Criterion	Description
1. New skill creation	An agent creates new skills by utilizing its current environmental resources, internal state, physical resources, and by integrating current skills from the agents repertoire.
2. Incorporation of new skills with existing skills	These new skills are incorporated into the agents' skill repertoire and form the basis from which further potential development can proceed.
3. Autonomous development of motivations	In a manner similar to its development of skills in Criterion 1 and 2, the robot develops its values and goals.
4. Bootstrapping of new skills	When the system starts, some skills rapidly become available.
5. Stability of skills	Skills persist over an interval of time.
6. Reproducibility	The same system started in similar initial states in a similar environment also displays similar ongoing emergence.

Table 2.1: Criteria for Assessing Robotic Ongoing Emergence, from [47].

learning object recognition, [18] uses the caregiver to bring the object close to the robot so that the object can be segmented on a disparity map). The caregiver can also give appropriate opportunities (e.g. orient the object so that it can be grasped). Finally the caregiver may manually guide the robot with compliant actuators [24] or trigger by speech command already acquired skills in order to learn a sequence [66].

- Imitation of human action can guide the robot towards learnable tasks faster than autonomous exploration. The most progressive (from the point of view of autonomy) approaches in imitation allow the system to recognize the relevant features of the action, [6]. This ability is not emergent as it is restricted to the choice from several possible pre-designed features. Still the system can choose autonomously the level of imitation. It can either learn exactly the trajectory or learn the action that leads to the recognized goal.

The third group of mechanisms focuses on the statistical learning and makes use of the Information Theory formalism. The main exploited principle here is the fact that the coupling of action back to the sensor introduces a structure in the sensory flow [35]. The authors call it "principle of information self-structuring": the ability of embodied agents to actively structure their sensory input and to generate statistical regularities in their sensory and motor channels. A similar idea was used in [28] in order to enable the system to introduce visual categories by the extraction of the image parts that are correlated to the own movement. The information-theoretical framework is often used in combination with evolution, e.g [30]. In this work the authors introduced the term "empowerment": agent-centric quantification of the amount of the control or influence that an agent has and perceives: the amount of information the agent can transmit to its sensors by performing a sequence of actions. Maximization of the empowerment can be used as a drive for the developmental process.

Finally, the forth group uses explicitly a value function. A value function defines a semantics (what is "good" and "bad") of the states and actions and is used to increase the likelihood that a "good" behavior reoccurs in a similar situation to experienced and evaluated one. The value function can be based on the sensor measurements, e.g. it can map the red color to "bad" and green to "good", or in a more biological example a sweet taste to "good" and a sour one to "bad" value. In this case it is called external value function. Alternatively, it can be based on the measurements generated internally in the system, e.g. such as a prediction error, often used as a novelty or curiosity reward. The analysis done in [43] shows the full spectrum of possible classifications of different value function. With respect to guiding the developmental process we see two classes:

- constant value function can show what has to be learned, e.g [56],

- dynamically changing value function can guide the behavior towards more complex task, e.g. [41].

The implementations of these approaches interest us the most, because they consider the system as a whole and not the learning of one isolated ability as it is often the case for morphology- or caregiver-based approaches. Further, in difference to the Information-Theory-based approaches, the value-function-based approaches use more complex test scenarios with non-trivial dynamics of the behavior changes. By analyzing these dynamics we can gain insight on how the design of the initial system influences the resulting developmental process. For this reason in the following sections we discuss these approaches in more details.

2.1.1 Development driven by Intelligent Adaptive Curiosity

The work done in [41] shows to our knowledge the first attempt to design and to analyze a task-unspecific developmental process. To bootstrap the development the system is provided with simple motor control primitives. For example in the experiment with the AIBO-dog the authors used a five dimensional continuous vector $M(t)$ with pan/tilt of the head direction, strength and angle of the leg bash, and crouching depth for biting primitive. A simple perceptive part $S(t)$ is a vector of sensor values. The pushing force or drive of the development is the **Intelligent Adaptive Curiosity** (IAC), that has a goal to maintain a high learning progress of the system. The progress is measured as the decrease of the prediction error. The prediction is done on the base of the segmentation of the sensorimotor space $SM(t)$ into the regions of low variance of the next sensory input $S(t+1)$. The system's policy is to choose an action from a region for which it expects a maximal learning progress and to choose a random action from time to time (ϵ-greedy policy in terms of reinforcement learning).

Equipped with this initial design (motor primitives, perceptive input, reward function and algorithm for segmentation of sensorimotor space into predictive chunks) the system shows a typical, stably reproducible, pattern of development. It starts with just looking around and finishes with coordinated looking and bashing towards the "bashable" object. In-between the system concentrates on a particular motor primitive that provides the highest learning progress. The most important point about this system is that the development is task independent.

2 State of the Art

The learning of object affordances and the coordination of looking with other actions was not explicitly pre-designed in the system, but emerged from the design of the intrinsic curiosity reward.

The main limitation of the system is the simplicity of the used representation. The acquired segmentation is valid only for the static environment seen during the experiment. It can not generalize to the changes in the environment. The learnt segmentation is not used directly in the control architecture, but only for the calculation of the value function. The authors see the increase of the representational complexity as a necessary step and propose an extension in the direction of a reinforcement-learning framework that we describe in the next section.

2.1.2 Intrinsically motivated Reinforcement Learning

One of the most extensively used frameworks for behavior control and learning by trial-and-error is the reinforcement learning (RL), [54]. This formalism uses pre-designed action primitives $a(t)$, a state representation $s(t)$, and a reward function $r(t)$. What is learned is an approximation of either the state-value function $V(s(t))$ or the action-value function $Q(s(t), a(t))$. The first one defines the maximal possible future reward that can be acquired starting from the state $s(t)$. The second one defines the maximal possible future reward that can be acquired starting from the state $s(t)$ if the first executed action is $a(t)$. The learning of the action-value function is preferred to the state-value function because it does not require the search over all actions that can be performed in every state. If the system knows the state-value or action-value function, then the action selection is straightforward. The action is chosen according to a greedy policy. If the state-value function is known, then a greedy action is the one that appears the best after a one-step search on the state-value function. If the action-value function is known, then we can simply take the action that maximizes the action-value function. As the future return is already calculated into the value functions, the greedy policy is sufficient to ensure the best reinforcement in the future without making a search in the tree of all possible action consequences. This is the main achievement of the reinforcement learning framework.

However the framework also has several limitations:

1. The expected future reward is calculated with the help of an artificial construct of the discounting rate: reward that lies further in the future is weighted by a smaller rate.

2. The system can build the policies from initially designed actions, but can not optimize the primitive actions themselves. The good choice of the action and state representation is crucial for the success of reinforcement learning.

3. The reward function has to be designed to match the task. For complex tasks it can become a non-trivial problem.

Recently attempts were made to overcome the last two limitations. In [54] the authors introduce an intrinsically motivated RL in order not to design a task-specific reward function. They also use a concept of options in order to have learnable modules available for behavior organization besides pre-designed action primitives.

An option is described by an initiation set, a transition probability model, a termination set, and an option policy. Every time an agent observes a new salient event it creates an option that achieves this salient event. The value function can take as an argument the whole option and the agent can choose to execute an option policy (authors call it "skill") in the same way as it can choose a primitive action. Thus with the help of options an agent can plan on a higher abstraction level. The fact that the option achieves the salient event is not coded into the reward function (as it would be the case for the policy learning in the classical RL), but into the termination set. The reward is a combination of extrinsic reward and intrinsic reward. The extrinsic reward is the reward the system gets for achieving a particular state as in the classical RL. The intrinsic reward is proportional to the error in prediction of the salient event done according to the option for this event. Thus the options used in [54] can be seen as a way to segment the sensorimotor space into predictor-controller pairs as presented in [41].

The segmentation is based on two facts. First, the internal action-value function of options takes into account only the extrinsic reward. It means that the adaptation of the option is independent of the segmentation that uses predictivity of the salient event. In the course of development the predictivity changes but it has an effect only on the intrinsic reward used on the higher level of action/option selection, not on the level of the option policy. Thus the option-specific controller can be stably learned. Second, the prediction model of an option is updated only if the action is a greedy action for this option. Thus the coherence of the predictor-controller pair is assured.

The authors experimentally show that the usage of options and intrinsic motivation speeds up the learning of a specific task. "Speeds up" means here that the system needs to experience a smaller number of task-specific rewards to learn the task. The dynamics of the developmental process is structured by the scenario. Some salient events are easy to produce and thus occur at earlier stages of the learning. These events become soon predictable and not reinforcing any more. Other salient events require a whole sequence of actions to be done and thus such events occur at later developmental stages.

Although the results are promising, some simplifications used in this approach are critical. The experiment is done in a simulation only. The action has no time dynamics, is always successful, and the reaction is directly measurable at the next time-step without measurement noise. Everyone who worked with a real hardware in the real-time scenario knows that these assumptions are not realistic.

The design of the learning also has some points to be criticized :

- the decision on what is salient is made by the designer and is innate, the system can not increase the set of salient events,

- the salient events can play the role of subgoals only for a restricted class of goals, not always a subgoal can be associated to some salient event,

- the only possible exploration is the random one, and

- the extrinsic reward defines the option-specific policy and thus it is not clear what would happen if the system uses several rewards or if the options are not needed to get the final extrinsic reward.

2 State of the Art

2.1.3 Declarative learning with Discrete Event Dynamic Systems

The work described in the previous section show that the pre-designed structure of behavior organization simplifies the learning. These idea is further developed in [21]. Pendant to "options" are the "behavior schema". Similar to options, schemas capture three facts:

1. possible transitions between the states with the help of the controllers (pendant to the option policy),

2. the set of controllers and schemas available to this schema (pendant to the initial set of an option),

3. and set of absorbing states (similar to the termination set of an option).

The crucial difference to options is the choice of the state representation. Instead of a traditional vector of sensor readings the authors use the state of the error function of controllers. This state can be undefined, converging, or converged (absorbing state). For example instead of representing the distance to the object in the state vector $s(t)$ the authors encode the state of the reach controller. It is undefined if no object is present, it converges if the distance decreases, and is converged (in absorbing state) if an object is reached. On this example it becomes clear why we make a parallel between the initial set of an option and the set of controllers available to schema: the schema can be initialized whenever for some of its controllers the error function is defined. We can interpret the set of absorbing states as a prediction for the results of executing a schema. Contrary to an option, which predicts a single salient event, different absorbing states are possible for a schema. The state prediction is not used by the framework. The reward is directly calculated from the tactile sensor and the novelty of the vision sensor.

The big advantage with respect to classical RL is that the state abstraction used in [21] not only effectively reduces the dimension of the state space but also allows a new way of time representation. Instead of representing the system's state one represents the state of the dynamical processes going on in the system. We refer later to this approach as the Discrete Event Dynamic Systems (DEDS) schema.

There exist successful DEDS-based implementations of the learning on different levels, [26]. In [25] the authors learn the policy that combines basic controllers to a schema. In [46] the authors show how using abstract schema the system can learn the needed parameters for particular instantiation of the schema. In [21] the authors focus on the declarative learning, it means the learning of the better abstract schema. They propose to observe the entropy of the state-action transition distribution in the current policy. The high entropy means that the used representations are not enough to model the environment. In this case a new controller and thus a new state is introduced. For example in the grasping scenario the robot discovers that the presence of the human is correlated to the successful touching of the object that was out of reach (because the human holds the object out). Then the "localize-reach-grasp" schema is augmented by a "search" controller to test the assertion that a human is present. The state space representation is accordingly augmented by the state of the search controller. In this way active perception is nicely incorporated in the framework. Unfortunately different types of learning were not yet integrated into one scenario with simultaneous learning.

2.1.4 Comparison of developmental processes for different architectures

By setting a particular control architecture the designer defines how the system interacts with the environment and what are the free parameters and free structures that can be learned. In this section we compare the presented approaches first with regard to the dynamics of interaction and then with regard to the dynamics of changing knowledge representations.

Approach/ criteria	IAC	Intrinsic RL	DEDS-schema
Segments sub-policy exists?	no	yes, guided by the overall extrinsic reward	yes
What defines a segment?	stable prediction for $S(t+1)$ from $SM(t)$	salient event (sensor space) as termination set	the attractor of controller
System autonomously adds new segment?	yes, splits segment to decrease the variance of prediction	yes, adds new segment for not predicted salient event	yes, adds new controller if the state-representation is not sufficient to define a stable policy
What has to be pre-designed?	the thresholds of allowed prediction variance	salient events	controllers and error functions
Task specific design?	no	depends on generality of extrinsic reward and salient events	depends on generality of extrinsic reward and available controllers

Table 2.2: Sensorimotor segmentation in different learning approaches.

The diagrams of Figure 2.1 visualize the design properties of different approaches. All these approaches segment the flow of interaction between the agent and its environment and use the segments to create policies. In Table 2.2 we summarize the features of different ways to segment the sensorimotor space. During the developmental process the interaction flow between the agent and the environment has the following attractors:

- **IAC:** The sensorimotor region where the separation into smaller region leads to lower variance of the sensory input at the next time step.

- **Intrinsic-RL:** Salient events that are not yet predictable, but are achievable with a sequence of actions that leads to extrinsic reward.

- **DEDS-schema:** Absorbing states of controllers that build greedy policy for the reward function.

With the help of these attractors we can analyze the stability of the learning:

2 State of the Art

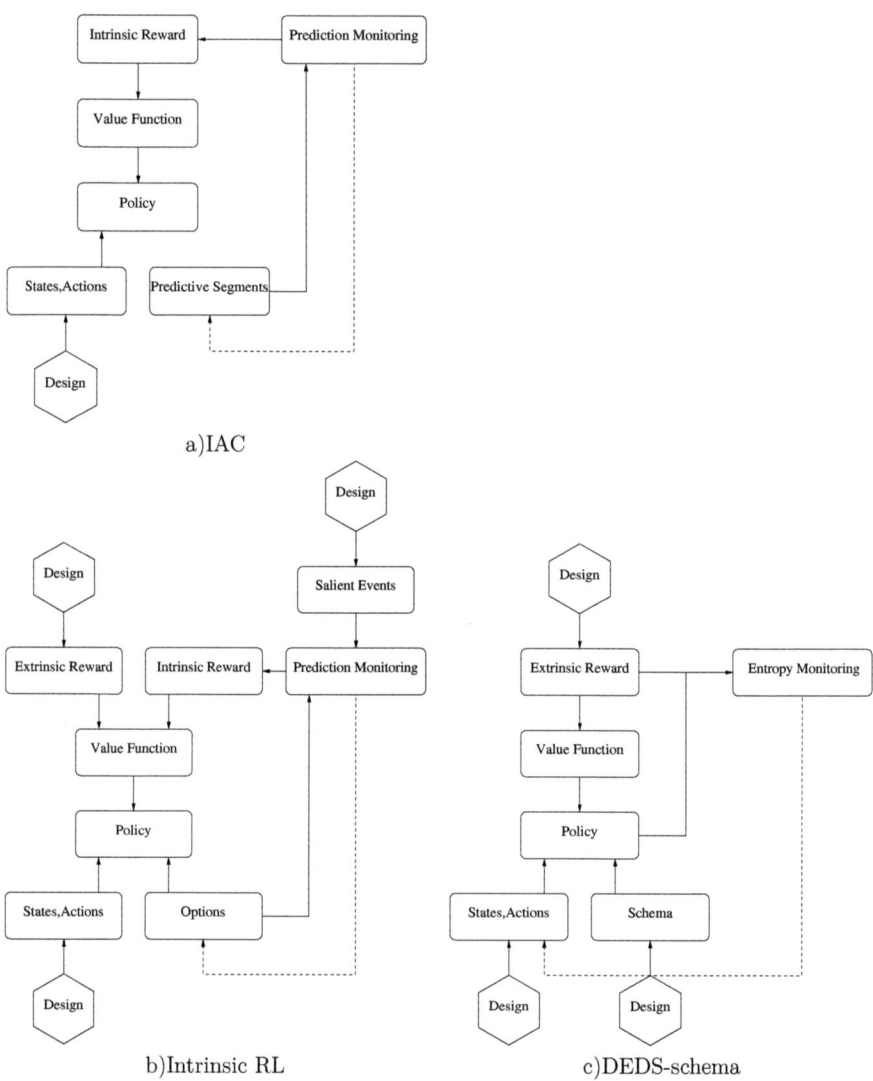

Figure 2.1: Diagrams of different system designs. The arrows describe the dependencies over the used representations and structures (not the data flow). The dashed line shows how new structures are created. a) Intelligent Adaptive Curiosity, [41]. b) Reinforcement learning with intrinsic motivation, [54]. c) Declarative knowledge learning in Discrete Event Dynamic Systems (DEDS) schema, [21].

1. Does the system learn the noise? In the sense that if the action-response pattern is not causal, but random, does the system try to learn it?

2. What happens if the system makes an observation of an interaction pattern that contradicts the learnt segmentation?

3. How the learning of the segmentation is decoupled from the learning of the segment-specific controllers?

To 1) (learning noise): IAC system tries to learn the random interaction flow only after the causal flow regions are learned. Intrinsic-RL: The random salient event is always attractive for the system. However, whether the system executes the option to achieve this event or not depends also on the extrinsic reward for this salient event. DEDS makes the assumption that the high entropy is caused not by noise but by missing sensor information or missing state representation, i.e. missing controller. Thus it tries to learn and to control the noise.

To 2) (plasticity/stability): IAC splits the segment further, without considering a possibility of having observed an outlier. Intrinsic-RL changes a prediction inside of the option with small learning rate: it averages over the seen data. DEDS makes a statistical evaluation by calculating the entropy of the state-action transition distribution. Thus the observation is only important if it affects the policy.

To 3) (decoupled learning): IAC does not learn controllers, only the overall policy. Intrinsic-RL allows only one policy to get to the salient event, which defines the segment. The option's internal policy is driven by extrinsic reward and is thus completely decoupled from segmentation. DEDS: The error function of the controllers is pre-designed, not learned. The segmentation is tightly coupled to the controllers because the state is defined by the controller's error function.

In sum, all discussed approaches aim at a segmentation of the sensorimotor flow of interaction between the system and the environment. The acquired segmentation allows for discretization and the usage of the classical reinforcement learning for Markov Decision Processes. The choice of segmentation criteria leads to different stability properties of learning. The advantage of IAC and Intrinsic-RL is that these approaches do not attempt to learn to control a noisy environment. The price that they pay for having such advantage is the low flexibility of control structures.

The IAC and IRL approaches formulate the developmental drive explicitly as striving for better prediction. The DEDS approach instead uses implicitly the necessity to disambiguate the situation as the drive of the development. Observation of the ambiguity in control allows to resolve the mismatch between the design of the reward and the initial design of the state/action representation (see Figure 2.1). This refinement of the representations together with the usage of abstract knowledge transfer and the usage of the controllers superpositions create a high potential for further success of the DEDS framework.

Although the principles, the guidelines, the constraints, and the requirements became more and more clear in the last decades, the implementations of the systems that display truly autonomous development are rare. The complexity of practical problems forces researchers either to introduce short-cuts (predesign the parts that should be learned) or to turn to simple toy problems. The fundamental principles of behavior organization have still to be understood.

2 State of the Art

For this reason the researchers in robotics are looking for inspiration in psychology and neurobiology.

2.2 Psychology

The two most prominent psychologists who investigated the drives and mechanisms of the child's development were Piaget and Vygodsky.

2.2.1 Drives of child's development according to Piaget

Piaget described behavior organization with the help of the notions "schema" and "operation". A schema is an abstraction of a stimulus-reaction association. An operation is an action on higher mental level, e.g. mental reflection or logical analysis. Piaget postulates that the schemas develop through assimilation and accommodation. Assimilation is an interpretation of an unknown stimulus via a known schema. For example a child knows the schema to suck on the mother's bosom and later assimilates the schema to suck on a bottle. Accommodation is a change of an existing schema. For example as the child changes the sucking to drinking. Acquisition of the concept of "wind" gives another, more abstract example of assimilation and accommodation. The child questioned in the Piaget's study explained that the wind comes from waving trees. Here the child assimilates the known schema "waving hand makes wind". Confronted with the fact that there also exists wind on the sea, the child needs to change the schema of causal relations, i.e. to make accommodation. Piaget postulated that the developmental drive is equilibration - a drive to obtain a balance between the schemas and the environment. According to Piaget the development takes place in four stages described in Table 2.3.

Stage	Description
Sensorimotoră (Birth-2 years)	Egocentric; acquires pragmatic intelligence; object permanence, symbolic schemas
Pre-operational (2-7 years)	Still egocentric; uses symbols but yet no hierarchies (no class inclusion)
Concrete operational (7-11 years)	Can think logically about objects and events.ă Decentration possible (more than one aspect, no visual dominance)
Formal operational (11 years and up)	Can think logically about abstract propositions and test hypotheses systematically. Becomes concerned with the hypothetical, the future, and ideological problems.

Table 2.3: Developmental stages according to Piaget.

The principle of equilibration can explain the acquisition of a consistent knowledge base represented by schemas. However Piaget's work did not pay enough attention to the question how the schemas are used for behavior control. Also in the case of the mental operations Piaget was interested in logical reasoning for building a consistent world model, but not for behavior control. Nowadays the researchers in robotics are aware of the fact that construction of the world-model is not sufficient for intelligent behavior in dynamic environments. From this perspective it is clear that the essential question of the development: "How does the acquired knowledge enhance the control of the behavior" was not sufficiently well approached by Piaget's theory. That is why it does not provide a sufficient explanation for the transition from sensorimotor stage to symbolic stages.

2.2.2 Principles of development according to Vygodsky

The theory of Piaget is well known. The concepts of schemas and developmental stages found its adepts in the robotic community ([2], [32]). The work of Vygodsky is less known. It is mainly reduced to the concepts of social learning and the zone of proximal development. Here we would like to discuss less known ideas of Vygodsky on what he called "the system of the higher psychological/mental functions" [59].

While Piaget described what a child can or cannot do at a particular age, Vygodsky was interested in transition from "cannot" to "can". To explain the transition from sensorimotor to symbolic stages Vygodsky introduced the concept of mediation.

Mediation can be shortly described as breaking the entity of a stimulus-response loop by introducing a symbol to represent a possible answer. In this process the lower ("natural" in Vygodsky's words) layer of established stimulus-response reaction is rewired by the higher layers. While the selection on the lower level is the "winning the access to the motor space", the selection on the higher level is the "winning the access to closing a particular stimulus-action loop".

The role of psychological tools for the control of the behavior is to introduce a media (symbols) to support the selection process. Vygodsky describes an experiment that shows the transition of the control from a natural to a mediated level. In this experiment a child is asked to remember which piano tab to push for shown stimuli. If the child solves the problem directly, without any tools for memorization, then the solution is coded directly into the sensorimotor loops. One observed that if the child is uncertain, then it moves its hand back and forth before it could decide which tab to push. If the child uses helping pictures that it can attach to the tabs, then there is no "testing" hand movement. The selection happens on the level of symbolic associations between the shown and the attached pictures, not on the motor level. The motor system is only executing the action chosen on the symbolic level.

The above example pin-points the main idea: the symbols are not the tools for building a world model, but the tools for behavior control. Vygodsky sees also the speech as a psychological control tool that is first applied to the child from outside by the parents, then applied by the child to parents and finally applied by the child to its own planning routines, first as "external speech" (children's commentary to what they are doing) and next as mental speech - thought.

Consequently Vygodsky characterizes the developmental process as a change of used control structures: "Perestrojka of needs, goals, values constitutes the basis of developmental stages". He proposes the same stages for development of different psychological tools (see Table 2.4). In contrast to Piaget these stages are not coupled to a particular age because they correspond to functional distinction and not to phenomenological description. Vygodsky's stages characterize the same 'internalization' process applicable to different abilities at a different age.

Since Piaget and Vygodsky the developmental psychology has become a separate strong

2 State of the Art

Stage	Counting	Writing	Speech
Natural (mechanical repetition)	Counting gestures without knowing the result	Gesture with a pen (pierce to draw a mosquito)	Speech as a tool to manipulate other ("mama" means "mama put me up")
External (natural function but related to a goal)	Counting with the help of fingers	Drawing = object (turn a page to see the back of object)	Egocentric or private speech (counting 1-2-3-Go! in order to jump)
Internal abstraction	Symbolic counting without fingers	Symbolic writing in order to remember	Inner speech linked to concepts and thoughts used for self-control

Table 2.4: Developmental stages for higher psychological functions.

branch of psychology. Much interesting work has been done in specific domains of development of language and gestures, walking, and imitation. However we have to be careful about using the results from psychology. Psychology often aims at describing and modeling observed data. Unfortunately a phenomenological behavior description gives often a wrong idea about the processes that generate the observed behavior.

In the next section we look at the intelligent system not from outside but from inside with the help of the research done in neurobiology.

2.3 Neurobiology

Artificial systems can profit from the findings in neurobiology on different levels. One can take inspiration from the brain in order to improve the computer chips and the hardware. One can adapt the principles of low-level information processing from the spiking neurons and cortical columns. As we are interested in system aspects, we will consider the level of integration of different brain subsystems to a developing system.

2.3.1 Brain development in ontogeny and phylogeny

The embryo development (ontogeny) undergoes similar stages as evolution (phylogeny). This fact inspired the researchers to ask if the mental development on the life-time span also follows the evolutionary changes in the brain.

An attempt to compare a child directly with our ancestors, human-like apes, shows that the similarities are only shallow. The same observable behavior of a child and an ape is often produced by functionally different control mechanisms, [59]. Both a child and an ape can learn to use a stick to get an inaccessible object. But the ape learns only if the stick and the object are in the same field of view, whereas the child can switch the gaze direction and use the stick which lies far apart.

Much more useful is the comparison of developmental and evolutionary processes directly

2.3 Neurobiology

on characteristics of the brain architecture [53]. It has been shown indeed [49] that the older cortical areas have adult-like patterns of responsiveness earlier than evolutionary younger parts. The older cortical regions (hippocampical cortex and paleocortex) are less specialized: they have lower resolution in the representation of the sensory input and get inputs from all modalities. Whereas the younger cortical areas (primary motor and sensory areas) are more detailed and devoted to one particular modality. Basing on these observations authors in [53] propose to bootstrap the incremental development with the help of an "evolutionary older" brain-part. This part provides 1)fast action-perception loop without fine resolution and 2)control and coordination of "newer" specialized sensor processing.

Strikingly, most approaches in developmental robotics follow exactly the opposite way. They start with specific behavior with high resolution on the motor and sensory side and learn abstract concepts and associations that fuse different sensory modalities.

2.3.2 Models for organization of learning in the brain

The above stated hypothesis about the propagation of the learning from general to specialized control is supported by existing models for organization of the learning in the brain, e.g. Haruno-Kawato's heterarchical model for reinforcement learning in cortico-striatal loops [22].

According to this model, in the early stage the learning uses the coarse description of the situation (limbic and associative part of the cortico-striatal loop). Later stages of the learning focus on more detailed descriptions in the motor part of cortico-striatal loops. The advantage of this model is that the gradual propagation of prediction error facilitates the learning.

Next we describe another point where neurobiological models are considerably different from the robotics applications. Most approaches in developmental robotics support only one type of learning in only one part of the system. In contrast, neurobiology shows that in the brain there are multiple structures that are all learning in qualitatively different ways. Doya's model [14] proposes the following mapping between brain structures and the type of learning, see Figure 2.2:

- cerebellum - supervised learning of internal models of the world;

- basal ganglia - reinforcement learning of action selection by the evaluation of environmental states;

- cerebral cortex - unsupervised learning of statistically efficient representation of the environment and the system.

Doya focuses on the reinforcement learning of the action selection in basal ganglia. The working hypothesis is that the part of this brain structure, the striatum, encodes the action value, i.e. the expected future reward if executing this action, whereas the neuromodulator dopamine encodes the error of reward prediction, [15]. This error is used for updating of the value function in accordance to the classical reinforcement learning theory. The dynamics of the dopamine release was shown to be modeled sufficiently good by this theory. Although the hypothesis about the role of dopamine in action value learning is well accepted, it is worth to mention that the value or reward is coded by several areas in the brain and the role of dopamine can vary across this different areas [63].

2 State of the Art

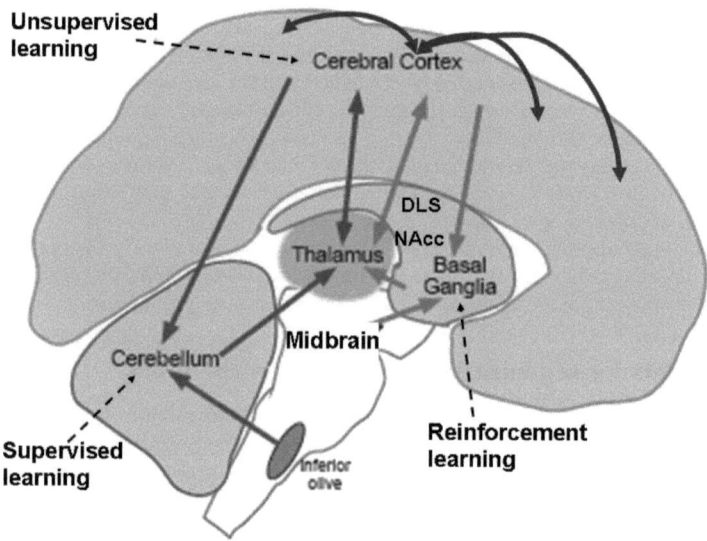

Figure 2.2: Multiple learning structures, adapted from [15]. The parts of the basal ganglia (NAcc - nucleus accumbens, DLS - dorsolateral striatum) that learns different types of behavior communicate mainly over a spiral interconnections to midbrain and thalamocortical loops.

The brain organization is much too complex that we could go into details of the reward processing by the brain. We would like however to emphasize some features which we consider as important for us.

First of all, the neurobiologists rarely speak about reward representation in one isolated area, but often about processing in loops. For example one of the reward related loops, called limbic circuit, [1], contains amongst others the hypothalamus, which participates in homeostatic control of the body functioning; the amygdala, which is a crucial structure for signaling the input relevance needed in conditional learning; the ventral part of the basal ganglia, which are thought to control the actions selection; the thalamus, which gates the input to the cortex; and several cortical regions, which participate in the storage of the experience in an appropriate form. If we want to learn from this feature of the brain architecture, then we have to a allow coupled dynamics of changing needs, changing behavior and changing internal representations and focus on coupling between these parts.

Second, the different areas that participate in the reward representation and processing can be correlated with different levels of behavior complexity but there is no explicit hierarchy between these levels. For example one part of the basal ganglia, nucleus accumbens, is crucial for the conditional learning, while another part, dorsolateral striatum is crucial for the instrumental learning [63]. The interaction between these parts occurs rather over spiral connections between the basal ganglia and midbrain as well as the thalamo-cortical loops, not over direct communication, see Figure 2.2. This structure inspires us to use a design with parallel multiple reward representations and parallel control loops, rather than a strict behavior hierarchy.

A final issue about reward is the following: the brain researchers differentiate between 'liking' or hedonic pleasure as mediated by opiodes and hedonic circuit, and 'wanting' or predictive and motivational signals as mediated by dopamine [5, 63]. This fact supports the assumption that there exists an initial pre-designed reward system together with a motivational system for learning to refine the initial value system, [31].

2.4 Summary

In this chapter we discussed existing approaches that address the dynamics of developmental process

- as guided by incremental changes on the morphological level (maturation of sensors and actuators),
- as guided by the social interaction with a teacher,
- as guided by the improvement of interaction with environment from information-theoretical point of view,
- and as guided by the value function (by extrinsic reward or by changes in the intrinsic reward)

These mechanisms have been observed in psychology (section 2.2) and have been proved to be useful in technical implementations (section 2.1). Still there exists no artificial system that exhibits truly open-ended development. It means no system that would continuously acquire new skills (physical or mental) and integrate them with existing skills (see criteria for ongoing emergence in table 2.1).

In our analysis of existing approaches (section 2.1.4) we observed that the critical step in the design of the developing system is the decision how the segmentation of the sensorimotor space is done. The purpose of the segmentation is to introduce abstraction units (prediction model, option, schema) used for non-reactive control, e.g. for planning. On one extreme end we have the high adaptivity of the units without true abstraction and support of the hierarchy building (IAC approach). While on the other extreme we have an architecture that allows for a hierarchy at the price of no possibility to refine the basic elements (IRL approach). The DEDS approach has an advantage of allowing for both units refinement and hierarchy. Another big advantage of this approach is the coupling of the reactive controllers with planning. Unfortunately, as every reinforcement learning approach, it optimizes only one specific reward and it is not clear if it can lead to a task-unspecific open-ended development.

Exactly these two requirements: being task-unspecific and open-ended have a high priority in our research on developing systems. For this reason we propose to change the view-point. We do not fix a particular task as the end-point and ask how the system could develop to this point. Instead we look at the system as a starting point and ask how we have to design it in the way that existing abilities support further development of the system. In other words we ask what is a

2 State of the Art

good system design for bootstrapping of the development. In our work we will make an attempt to follow the neurobiological principles discussed in Section 2.3 and use the multiple layers of the control architecture, the propagation of the learning from general to specific behavior, and the multiple structures for the learning of regularities in system-environment interaction.

3 Design of Developing Systems

The developmental approach supposes that the innate bootstrapping consists at least of a self-motivation or value system, an abstraction and anticipation system, as well as innate behaviors, see e.g. [34], [8] and Figure 2.1. The design of these parts constraints what the system can learn and what the resulting behavior will be. For this reason we devote this chapter to design questions before in the next chapter we move on to realizations.

We discuss first how we should choose the rewards used in the value system so that the developmental process does not stagnate. We consider then what we have to take into account in implementation of innate behaviors if we want that they favor the developmental process. Finally, we formulate the requirements on the abstraction system. Here again we focus our attention on the open-endness of the development. We ask how the system uses already present abilities for the acquisition of new ones. This is different from the question "how the abilities would emerge from tabula rasa" discussed in earlier times of Developmental Robotics with a radical "no pre-design" philosophy. The idea of incremental building helps not only to structure the research. It also emphasizes that we want that "learning" becomes "development", in the sense that not only quantitative knowledge accumulation in one subsystem is possible, but also qualitative changes in the overall system behavior, e.g. extension from reactive behavior to expectation driven behavior.

3.1 Design of a value system: specific versus unspecific reward

In the literature several proposals for the design of reward have been made varying from very sensor-close and specific, e.g. red objects, [56], to very sensor-far and unspecific, e.g. learning progress, [42], novelty and predictability, [36].

The specific rewards are easy to implement, but they can lead to severe symbol grounding problems. Indeed, the value function is the last mean for the system to self-monitor its behavior. Thus the 'recognition' errors in measurement of the value function are fatal. Still such errors can easily happen, similar to object recognition errors, if the designer reduces the reward to one source and one context only. For example in [51] a "social reward" is given if the human comes closer to the robot. However, in a natural environment the human could come closer to the robot because the human is angry and not because he wants to reward the robot.

An additional issue of specific reward is its locality. It rewards the end-point without rewarding the way towards it. Thus it can not help to find a temporary extended strategy. For example associating red objects with reward does not help to grasp a red object from an inaccessible position.

In contrast, unspecific rewards cover large parts of the behavior space, it means the space spanned by all possible sensory inputs and all possible motor commands available for chosen

3 Design of Developing Systems

hardware. The unspecific rewards can provide the evaluation of unknown situations not foreseen by the designer. Such an evaluation can considerably speed up the exploration compared to a pure random search. For example, the work presented in [42] uses the learning progress as an unspecific reward. The results of this approach confirm that specific behaviors can emerge from unspecific reward.

Except for qualitative reviews of approaches in developmental robotics, e.g. [34], there exists yet no well-established methodology for comparing different designs. We propose a simple empirical consideration which can help to design a motivational system.

It makes no difference whether one pre-designs some reactive, innate, task-specific solution or a self-motivation system if the reward chosen for motivation occurs only in the situations which correspond to this very task-specific solution.

In other words: with the introduction of the self-motivation system one can gain more adaptivity only if the reward used in this system covers more possible patterns of system-environment interaction, than the patterns produced by reactive behavior.

From the point of view of adaptation it means that the system can adapt if it can go back to the general evaluation (general description of "good" and "bad") once the specific evaluation (specific strategy) turns out to be wrong.

Consequently, for our goal of increasing adaptivity of a reactive system unspecific, general, grounded rewards are a better design choice. This is validated by an experiment that will be described in section 4.1. It does not necessarily mean that there is no need for specific rewards, it only means that they are probably playing a different role, e.g. for conditioning.

We would like to make a short notice on the influence of the value system on the control system. The classical reinforcement learning considers only one reward source and the aim of the control system is to optimize the actions as to maximize this reward. However, a complex system such as a robot interacting with a human, has to satisfy multiple, conflicting needs. While one variable is driven to an optimal value, another variable is necessarily pushed out of the optimum. Another cause of unavoidable deviations from an optimum is the fact that in many cases the reward comes only with a time delay. Thus we need more flexible control than a classical control to a stable set-point or an optimal value, see Figure 3.1.

We favor the idea of homeostatic control in the sense of Ashby [23]: "Homeostasis is a process by which the certain variables, the essential variables, remain within given limits." In our case the variable to keep within given limits is the average amount of the reward. The system is allowed to execute not optimal actions, but it should not be the case that the system does not get a particular reward for a long time period. In order to monitor the average reward and to provide this information to the action selection mechanism we introduce the vector of needs $\vec{N}(t)$. They grow in absence of rewards $\vec{R}(t)$ and decrease in presence of rewards. This coupling can be modeled for example by following dynamic equation:

$$\tau_N d\vec{N}/dt = \vec{N}(t) .* \left(\vec{R}_0 - \vec{R}(t) \right),$$

where .∗ means component-wise multiplication, the positive time constant τ_N regulates the rate of changes in N and the constant vector $\vec{R}_0$ is the desired reward average. Can such a dynamics have stable solutions other than a constant need level with a constant reward $\vec{R}(t) \equiv \vec{R}_0$? The answer is yes. For example, if the dynamics of the reward acquisition can be modeled by the

3.2 Design of innate behaviors: provide favorable interaction

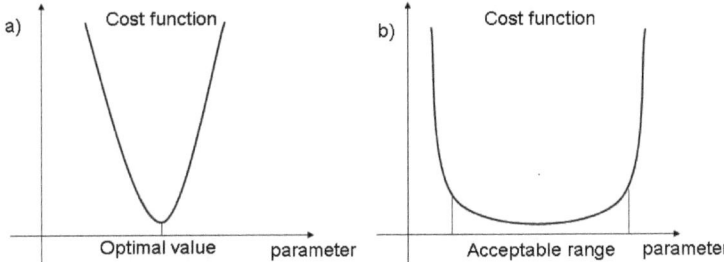

Figure 3.1: Optimal parameter setting versus homeostatic control. a) The system is controlled to a fixed set-point where the costs are minimal. b) Homeostasis: the system is allowed to take a range of states as long as the average costs are not too high.

equation $\tau_R d\vec{R}/dt = -\vec{R}(t).*(\vec{N}_0 - W\vec{N}(t))$ then the resulting system

$$\begin{cases} \tau_N d\vec{N}/dt = \vec{N}(t).*\left(\vec{R}_0 - \vec{R}(t)\right), \\ \tau_R d\vec{R}/dt = -\vec{R}(t).*(\vec{N}_0 - W\vec{N}(t)) \end{cases}$$

is a well-known Lotka-Volterra system that has been proved to have a stable periodic solution, see [64]. In [38] we analyze also other possibilities to model a homeostatic process by means of a dynamic system. The assumption that we can model the dynamics of the reward acquisition is surely unrealistic. But in this way we can see that the homeostatic control allows not only set-point solutions but also stable periodical solutions. In Section 3.3 we discuss in more detail how the mapping from the needs to the system's behavior can be organized.

3.2 Design of innate behaviors: provide favorable interaction

The evaluation of the situation can be encoded into the system in two ways. Above we discussed an explicit way - coding of the reward signal. An implicit way is to directly encode the reaction to the situation. A reader familiar with Braitenberg's vehicles, [10], can use his example for understanding this point: your can directly code your robot to turn towards the light, with no explicit coding of reward coming from the light. In the earlier times of Developmental Robotics the researchers argued against the pre-design per-se. In contrast, we support the idea of using known solutions whenever it is possible to encode them as fast, stable, and general reactive behaviors. The argument that the engineers can only roughly estimate the parameters in use (e.g. geometry of the robot) does not hold, because nowadays a number of algorithms exists for the parameter estimation. The implementation of higher level learning, in the sense of open-ended development, is only obstructed by argumentation against the pre-design of innate behaviors.

From the developmental perspective the goal of simple innate behaviors is to close the loop and to bootstrap the interaction with the environment. This interaction should be robust

3 Design of Developing Systems

in order to enable stable observations. The tracking of an object, for example, stabilizes the position of the object in the center of the image, so that the system can stably learn the object's visual properties (see Section 4.1 for a corresponding experiment).

Further we require that the bootstrapping involves the interaction with a human. The system should use a simple strategy that can motivate a human to provide a learnable interaction. Similar to the compliance control, that uses adaptiveness instead of perfect position control, the system should use the intelligence of the human that helps to fulfill the (may be even not intended) goal. We give an example below in order to clarify this point. If we bootstrap the system with grasping only at the accessible positions we can maybe optimize the grasping parameters. But if we bootstrap the system with **erroneous** grasping towards all objects, even those positioned far away, the system can learn not only to grasp, but also to request an object because the action of the system provokes the help of the user. For successful learning from interaction the system has to care about two aspects. First, it has to provoke a stable reaction of the user. Second, it has to make its internal states observable for the user so that he can interfere and correct the learning process. In the sections 4.2 and 4.3 we give the examples of implementations that actively 'use the user'.

Some approaches in developmental robotics, e.g. [42], design the initial behaviors as 'open-loops', i.e. the parameters of the behavior are set by a higher instance. We favor the closed-loop type, so that the innate behavior is an autonomous controller. For example, instead of the ability to move the gaze at a commanded position we start with the ability to track an object. Such a design has two advantages: first, the overall system architecture is more stable as the reactive layer can still act in absence of the higher layers; second this design prevents an artificial separation of 'action' from 'perception'. Instead we pursue the detachment of the higher mental concepts from the initially given sensorimotor loop in the course of development. Still for the generation of new behaviors we need direct access to the controllers. Thus we require that reactive behaviors have a continuous parameterization or accessible neighborhood that can be used for exploration.

3.3 Design of an abstraction layer: beyond reactivity

In the last two sections we discussed a reactive system that bootstraps the interaction with the environment on a fast time-scale and the value system that monitors the reward on a slow time-scale. With these two systems we create a basis for development of the abstraction layer on an intermediate time-scale that would allow a transition from a stimulus driven reaction to a stimulus expecting behavior.

3.3.1 Requirements for abstraction layer

Obviously the design of the abstraction layer and its building blocks (aka action and perception primitives, schemas, mental concepts, etc.) is one of the hardest problems in the current research on cognitive systems. This question can not be tackled in a sufficiently deep way within the scope of this work. What can be done as a first step of the design process is the clarification of goals and resulting requirements. While introducing an abstraction layer over a reactive one we request that:

3.3 Design of an abstraction layer: beyond reactivity

1. The abstraction layer is not blocking the reactive layer.

   One aim of incremental system building is to guarantee the robustness of the system. In the case of failure of a later added layer, the older layers have to be allowed to take over the control. There exist different possibilities to implement the take-over. For example, both layers can emit the commands with different priorities, so that the command with the highest priority inhibits all the other ones. With such a design, if one command is not emitted at all, this does not block another commands. Quite a different design possibility is to make first the decision which layer emits the command and then trigger the processing only in the selected layer. In this case, if the chosen layer is not able to emit the command, then no command can be emitted at all and the whole system is blocked. On these two examples we see the difference between inhibition and blocking. Hence, we have to carefully design the interaction between abstraction and reactive layers with respect to blocking.

2. There is autonomy to inhibit reactive actions.

   As explained above, this requirement does not contradict the first one. The abstraction layer is introduced in order to refine the initial reactive behavior with the help of learning. The enhanced behavior may require the inhibition of the innate reactions. An example of such reflex inhibition is provided by experiments with frogs, which are one of the simplest animals with a cortex. The frog is shown a black dot which looks like a fly. First the frog keeps on jumping to the dot, but then it can inhibit this unsuccessful reactive behavior.

3. There is autonomy to have a competition of multiple triggers.

   A reactive innate behavior is a fixed map that assigns to each trigger only one action. An abstraction layer represents a qualitative advantage only if it introduces new degrees of freedom and allows to choose which trigger can activate which action.

4. There is autonomy to act in absence of reactive actions triggers.

   Apart of inhibition of the innate reactions and the freedom to choose dynamically the triggers of the reactions, the behavior enhancement may require behaviors that can not be implemented with the help of sensory triggering. The exploratory behavior or searching are examples therefore.

5. There is an interface to the external commands.

   Since we aim at a robot acting in a human environment, it is natural to require that the human should be able to influence the robot's behavior by commands. This requirement has to be made explicit because it has direct consequences for the design of the system.

6. An abstraction can fuse information over time and over sensory channels.

   This requirement is a simple consequence of the fact that detection of correlations in time or between different sensory channels is the source of learning and robust processing of the abstractions of the sensory information.

7. An abstraction allows a generalization for evaluation of unknown behaviors and intelligent exploration.

The memorization of the experience in the abstraction layer can be subject to different optimization criteria. For example minimization of memory resources, minimization of the time needed for memory recall, etc. One of our aims is the qualitative enhancement of the behavior both in terms of efficient execution and efficient learning. For this reason we explicitly formulate the requirement on the generalization ability.

8. The system is suited to limited reaction time and memory resources.

   We aim at real-world applications running on autonomous robots. The abstraction layer introduces internal states and models that can get quickly out of sync with the changing real world. Thus the reaction time is limited, otherwise the action selection based on the old measurement becomes outdated. Not only the processing time, but also the memory consumption has to be carefully monitored, even though in the research phase we can use external computers for memorization and processing, hoping that in the future the hardware will be further improved so that we can do all processing on-board.

9. Processing can be reduced to a minimum for speed up in critical phases. It can be extended to parallel consideration of multiple possibilities in a phase of search or exploration of behavior.

   This requirement specifies one of the possible ways to assure fast reactions of the system. In this form it can be easier translated into design features.

10. An active testing/grounding procedure is available for created abstractions.

    The ability to create abstraction (aka mental concepts, schemas, perceptive/motor primitive etc.) relies on the ability to detect correlations that are relevant with respect to value function, e.g. correlations in time, in space, or over different sensory channels. We require that together with memorization of these correlations in form of abstractions, the system memorizes also the active procedure how it can reactivate the observation of these correlations. This procedure can be seen as testing or hypothesis resolution that is a necessary part of the information processing in the real-word environment.

One may notice that we do not include any requirements implied by planning, sequencing, and memorization, as these aspects are not in focus of our work. Indeed, we aim at the very first steps towards anticipation, not at a perfect planning system.

3.3.2 Formalization and abstraction types

In this section we take a very general view on the behavior generation in order to analyze the existing possibilities to introduce an abstraction layer.

Let us denote a reactive layer by B^r. A reactive layer consists of a number of simple local controllers L_i, $i \in [1, \ldots, N^r]$ and a competitive selection mechanism D (arbiter) in form of a non-linear dynamical system [4, 9]. Every controller implements a certain behavior as a mapping W_i^r from sensory input $S(t)$, including both external (camera, touch, audio, etc.) and internal (posture, forces, etc.) sensors, to the motor command $M(t)$. These controllers are local in the sense that they are independent of other controllers and get from sensory input all the information they need in order to produce an output. The behavior selection is solely

3.3 Design of an abstraction layer: beyond reactivity

based on a fitness value F_i that is provided by each controller. We denote by N^s the subset of the indexes of the selected controllers. In sum

$$B^r = \left\{ L_i : S(t) \stackrel{W_i^r}{\to} M(t), i \in [1,\ldots,N^r],\ D : F_i(t) \to N^s, N^s \subset [1,\ldots,N^r] \right\}.$$

The system that occupies a simple ecological niche can evolutionary adapt the reactive layer as to ensure its survival. However an agent within a complex ecological niche needs an explicit reward monitoring.

Let us denote by $R(t)$ the innate rewards and by $N(t)$ the corresponding needs of the system as described in Section 3.1. The extension of a reactive layer by an abstraction layer B^a introduces an autonomy of the system from the immediate action triggering encoded in the reactive layer. The abstraction layer aims at an explicit regulation of the system needs in difference to the reactive layer that implements an implicit regulation. From a general point of view an abstraction layer implements a mapping from the needs to the motor commands:

$$B^a = \left\{ A_j : N(t) \stackrel{W_j^a}{\to} M(t),\ j \in [1,\ldots,N^a] \right\}.$$

There exist different possibilities of interfacing the motor commands. An abstraction layer can add to a reactive layer a new controller that is driven exclusively by the abstraction layer or it can modulate a reactive controller:

$$W_j^a : W_i^r \stackrel{W_j^a}{\to} \widetilde{W}_i^r,\ i \in I^j \subset [1,\ldots,N^r],\ j \in [1,\ldots,N^a],$$

where I^j denotes a subset of indexes of the modified controllers. The classical reinforcement learning (RL) formalism is the realization of the first possibility (restricted to one need only) whereas more advanced versions of RL, e.g. [58] or the hybrid architectures e.g. [21] also use the modulation of the local controllers.

There exist also different possibilities to let the value system influence the building of the abstraction layer. We distinguish the following three ways:

1. evaluation of the system-environment interaction with respect to the reward,
2. optimization of the reward,
3. and optimization of internal processing on the abstraction layer.

In the following we discuss these ways in more details.

Creation of abstractions by structuring of the system-environment interaction with respect to reward

We consider first how the system can use the reward signal to structure its observations O. The system can observe its current state in sensorimotor space as well as causalities either between time-delayed measurements (predictive model) or between measurements in different channels (associative model). Both type of causalities can be formalized as expectations $S(t + \Delta t) \approx E(S(t), M(t))$ where E is the expectation model because the usage of an associative model can be seen as a process in time. In sum the observations are

3 Design of Developing Systems

$O = \{S(t), M(t), S(t + \Delta t) - E(S(t), M(t))\}$. As the observation space is huge, the most implementations aim at discretization of this space: $O \approx \bigcup_{d=1}^{N_d} O_d$, where O_d are clusters in one of described above spaces (sensory, motor, sensorimotor, or causality) and N^d is the number of necessary clusters. This is how the abstractions, i.e. action or perception primitives, come into the play. The aim of the clustering is to allow to memorize the evaluation of the system-environment interaction and use this information for behavior generation. The approaches in the vision domain focus on the processes of clustering of the sensory space that lead to robust differentiation with regard to a metric defined by value function [31]. Whereas the classical RL let the designer decide on the discretization $O = \left\{\bigcup_{k=1}^{N_d^s} S_k, \bigcup_{l=1}^{N_d^a} A_l\right\}$ with discrete sensory states S_k and actions A_l, hoping that it is appropriate for the learning of value function. As the RL deals with one-dimensional reward only, there exists no necessity to discretize the reward space. In simple cases the RL can also skip the discretization of the observation space, e.g. [50], [58], by solving the problem with only one adaptive control algorithm without introducing the abstractions.

We already mentioned that the structure of appropriate knowledge representation is one of the hardest problems in the actual research on cognitive systems. Here we do not ask what is the best way of knowledge representation, instead we make an overview on different possibilities seen from the perspective of a complete system that monitors its reward acquisition.

How can the memorized evaluation of the system-environment interaction be used for the behavior generation? Generally speaking, there exist two qualitatively different ways for behavior generation: either using a fixed policy or online inference and planning.

In the first case, which can be compared to habits, the action selection is done in one step without using explicit models for future prediction. For example, in the classical model-free RL the system chooses the action that directly maximizes the action-value function. Although there is no explicit future prediction, still the future is taken into account as the action-value function memorizes the maximum expected reward that can be achieved if starting with a particular action. This standard maximization approach can be replaced by ranking of memory according to the current need. This ranking can be applied to any type of observations: sensory, motor, or expectation-based. If we rank the sensory input, then the mapping W_j^a of the abstraction layer, introduced on page 29, can act as a filter on the reactive layer so that only the relevant sensory input can trigger an action. In the case of memorized motor commands the system can directly derive the priorities of memorized commands from the ranking. In the case of memorized expectations, the mapping W_j^a can activate the motor command that lets the system re-experience the situation where the expectation $E(S(t))$ is true. Chapter 4 will give the examples of implementations for some of described above mechanisms for behavior generation.

Our work does not consider explicit inference and planning. Still we would like to make a short comment on this second way of using memorization for behavior generation. In this case the system first uses the memorized evaluation in order to generate a valuable goal for the current need state. For example, from evaluation of red color as the 'good' one it sets the position of the red object as the target. In the second step it has to use prediction models and inverse models in order to generate a sequence of actions leading to the target. The planning steps may be time consuming and the action selection may be slower compared to the described above model-free mechanism of habits. However the model-based approach has an important advantage: as it separates the creation of goals and the policy search, it can adapt faster to the

3.3 Design of an abstraction layer: beyond reactivity

change of valuable goals. Indeed if only the goal is shifted, the predictive and inverse models for the actions need not to be re-learned. The inference and planning can be directly applied and find the new policy for the changed goal In contrast, in the case of memorized policy or habit, all the mappings have to be re-learned for the changed goal.

The decomposition of the system into the subsystems according to the reward metrics conceals the danger of an artificial credit assignment. Indeed, it is dangerous to give the credit to one subsystem only because the behavior of the system is the product of the activity of all subsystems. Considering our formalization of the abstraction layer with respect to this problem we would like to emphasize two points. First point is that the mappings realized by the abstraction layer are not exclusive. In contrast, they may run in parallel and thus they can share the credit. Second, we mentioned that instead of a central instance that judges what is the best mapping, one can use the ranking and prioritization. In this case the credit is distributed both in the monitoring and decision phases. Still we are aware of the fact that we may face the credit assignment problem as our system gets more complex.

Optimization of abstractions with respect to reward

A second qualitatively different way how the reward can influence the building of abstractions is the optimization [22]. The authors assume that there exists an initial clustering of the sensorimotor flow into the predictive models

$$\widehat{S}(t+1) = E_d(S(t), M(t)), d \in [1, \ldots, N^d],$$

where the $\widehat{S}(t+1)$ is the prediction of the sensory input and the N^d is the number of the models.

Each model is given the responsibility value which is inverse proportional to the prediction error of the model. The model with the smallest error thus has the highest responsibility. Every predictive model has its corresponding inverse model that is used for calculation of the action that leads to the maximal reward. The action proposals are weighted by the models responsibilities and summed up to the final action that is then executed. The weighted sum is a tractable operation in [22] because the used examples are the trajectory and the force control for the arm, and not a higher level of action description where summing up would make no sense. After the action is executed, the prediction models and corresponding inverse models are updated in a weighted manner: the higher is the responsibility of the model, the stronger is the update. As a result of the reiteration of differentiated updating, each pair of prediction and inverse models get specialized to a particular context. The sensorimotor space becomes segmented into a set of optimally tuned controllers for particular contexts. The predictive models tell what the current context is. Thus the system can do context recognition and switching of the controllers.

Optimization of abstractions with respect to internal processing on the abstraction layer.

Finally, the abstractions can be introduced as a result of the optimization of the operations to be executed on the abstraction layer, e.g. optimization of planning [58] or optimization of search [16]. As we already mentioned in the previous section, we aim at the very first steps from reactive to expectation driven behavior. Thus we focus first on the control-oriented

3 Design of Developing Systems

memorization as a mean for reward monitoring, and do not consider the next step of 'monitoring the monitoring'.

Comparison of different influence of value function on abstraction layer

Let us summarize the alternatives discussed above. First of all, the abstractions can result from structuring of the observation space with respect to reward. The system can memorize either clusters in sensor space, or clusters in sensorimotor space, or the expectation models that describe observed causalities. We call these cases respectively A:S:R, A:SM:R, and A:SE:R. Further, the abstraction clusters can follow the process of refinement of the prediction model driven by the optimization of action according to the reward. We call this case A:SE:O. Finally, the clusters can be a result of the optimization of the abstraction layer itself. This case is referred to as A:O:O. Figure 3.2 shows schematically the different types of abstraction building discussed above.

It depends on the final system implementation rather than on the used abstraction type if the requirements on the abstraction layer formulated in the previous section are fulfilled. For example the first two requirements on our list concern the coexistence of the abstraction layer parallel to a reactive one: the higher level has to be non blocking but able to inhibit the lower one. These properties are independent of the type of the abstraction. The desired loose coupling of different control layers can be achieved if we provide different priorities to the actions issued by different levels or if the higher levels do not set, but modify the parameters of the actions issued on the lower level.

In contrast, not all abstraction types allow for autonomy to act in absence of the reactive trigger (requirement 4). This requirement is fulfilled only by abstractions based on expectations (A:SE:O and A:SE:R). The clustering types A:SM:R and A:S:R provide only the possibility to make an evaluation of a present stimulus and thus can be used only for the competition between the triggers but not in the absence of the triggers.

A natural question arises whether we should prefer one type of abstraction building to another. In robotics there exists implementations of all types discussed above (see Section 2.1). Also during the experiments on animals one observes all types of learning [3]:

- stimulus-response (reinforcement learning, case A:SM:R);
- stimulus-response-stimulus (expectation learning, case A:SE:O);
- stimulus-response-good stimulus (reward expectation, case A:S:R);
- stimulus-stimulus (stimulus submission: bell is associated to food, case A:SE:R).

For this reason we believe that the discussion about the best suited abstraction type is contraproductive. Instead we investigate if we can incrementally build a system so that one type of abstraction supports the building of another abstraction type.

3.3.3 Development of the abstraction layer

As already mentioned in the introduction to this chapter, we see the development not as emergence of abilities from 'tabula rasa' but as an incremental process of the improvement of

3.3 Design of an abstraction layer: beyond reactivity

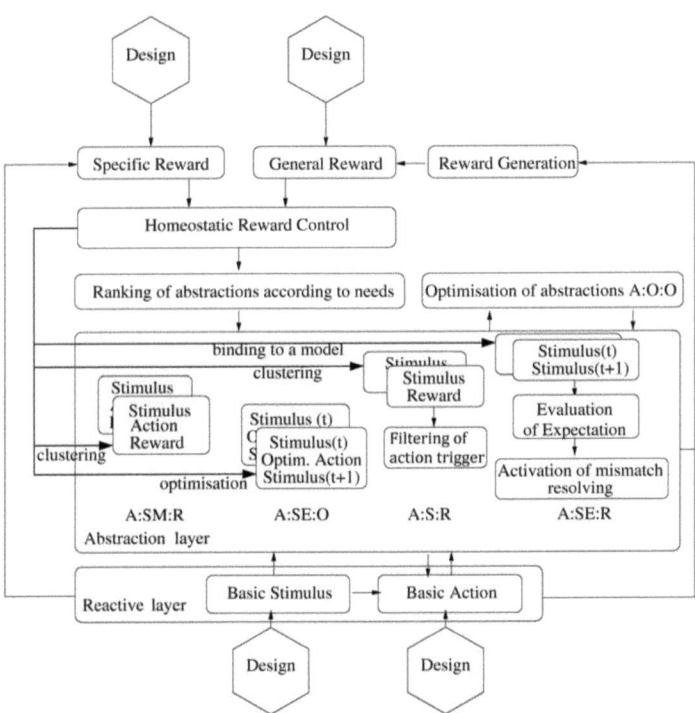

Figure 3.2: Design of the bootstrapping system for open-ended development. Different types of abstractions and the interfaces to the value system: direct evaluation and indirect link over optimization. See the text for more details.

33

3 Design of Developing Systems

a bootstrapping system. After we have formalized what the system can learn, it is now time to describe more formal the possibilities to learn incrementally. The question asked in this section is how the system builds up on its current abilities. We list below three cases to be analyzed with help of formalization introduced in the last section.

1. **Creating a favorable interaction with the environment.** In order to learn existing regularities the system e.g.
   - provides a stable sensor information for learning associations;
   - provokes learnable reactions of users or objects.
2. **Optimization.** The system optimizes the parameters of the controllers in use, e.g.
   - progresses from random motor babbling to coordinated action;
   - applies known skills in a new situation and optimizes the control parameters.
3. **Reorganization.** The system reorganizes its control structure and launches the skills that use newly learnt regularities, e.g.
   - concatenates sub-routines to a routine and builds a hierarchy;
   - uses the acquired concepts, models, abstractions as subject of higher mental functions (e.g. simulation, planning, attention control).

In the terms of the formalization done in the last section, to make a developmental progress according to case 1 it is sufficient that

- the system can create evaluative abstractions (type A:S:R, A:SM:R) for the general reward of being in interaction;
- the system can explore and optimize its interaction with the help of those evaluative abstractions;
- and the system can memorize in abstraction type A:SE:R the causalities experienced during the enhanced interaction.

In such a way, using evaluative abstractions A:S:R, and A:SM:R the system can make progress in acquisition of expectation-based abstractions A:SE:R.

The abstractions of the type A:SE:R can in their turn bootstrap the optimization (case 2 from the list on the top of this page). They can be used as an initial clustering or can define what has to be predicted in the A:SE:O abstraction type. The prerequisite is that the system is provided with an explicit local reward function or an implicit heuristics for optimization of the action for the refinement of A:SE:O abstractions.

Furthermore, the expectation-based abstractions A:SE:R can be used as a basis for reorganization (case 3 from the list on the top of this page). Indeed, with help of this abstraction type we can turn a reactive system into a goal-driven system by generating some behavior until the expectation is met. We recall that the expectations are generated starting from current observations: $S(t+1) \approx E(S(t))$ or $S(t+1) \approx E(S(t), M(t))$, where E is the expectation model. These expectations can be ranked according to the system need (see Section 3.3.2) and those with high ranking trigger the actions that can potentially lead to the re-experience of the expected situation. One may ask why do we need the current observations and the expectation models, why don't we let the system generate expectations by an internal process starting directly from needs? The advantage is that the gap between the current and expected situation stays small so that it could be potentially bridged by a behavior that does not require an extensive planning. We call such behaviors 'resolving the expectation mismatch'. The resolving behaviors can range from very simple and general to precise and complex. For example the expectation of particular visual feature can activate a random search with cameras or a more advanced modulation of attention. Similarly, the mismatch in audio channels can activate a simple user-directed behavior that requires the user to pronounce a new word (e.g. showing at the object) or it can trigger the system to pronounce the right word by itself. The link from expectation-based abstraction to the resolving behavior is crucial because it allows us to make a step from reactive to expectation-driven behavior. The essential difference to the reactive behavior is that the system has a local value to be monitored: the expectation mismatch. Thus it can judge on the local success and switch alternative resolving behaviors without monitoring a general reward that may be delayed. In difference to this closed loop, the abstractions of the type A:S:R and A:SM:R can only modify the reactive behavior in an open-loop manner.

The link from the expectations to the resolving behavior is especially important as it gives the system a possibility to re-enact the observation. The system can re-experience the situation were it observed and created the expectation model. Thus it can verify whether this model is appropriate as an observation used for memorization of the experienced reward and refine or correct the model.

The above analysis shows that different abstraction types create a synergy: the extension of the reactive system by simple abstraction types for general reward (A:S:R, A:SM:R) enhances the process of development of expectation-based types (A:SE:R, A:SE:O) for specific rewards. The expectation-based abstraction finally allows for a transition from a reactive to an expectation-driven behavior.

We would like to emphasize that we speak about enhancement of the development, not an emergence. Indeed the introduction of particular abstraction types requires specific interfaces to the reward system and to behavior generation as well as specific internal structure. In the next chapter we will give examples of how this specific structures can be implemented and how a reactive system can be extended by different types of abstraction.

3.4 Summary

In this chapter we discussed general design principles for bootstrapping a task-unspecific open-ended development.

We propose to start with a reactive layer that can work in absence of higher levels and can generate a robust, non-trivial interaction with the environment including basic interaction with humans.

Considering the second element of the bootstrapping - the value system - we propose to implement a homeostatic control of needs in contrast to reward maximization used in other developmental systems based on reinforcement learning. The homeostatic control is more suited to the system that has to satisfy multiple, conflicting needs. We favor the combination of specific

3 Design of Developing Systems

rewards (e.g. pleasure to activate sensory channels, pleasure to get human's approval) with general rewards (e.g. controllability, learning progress) that can recompense the intermediate steps from known situations with specific reward to new rewarding situations.

The third component of our proposal for the bootstrapping is the abstraction layer which is an initial structure to memorize the interaction with environment in relation to experienced reward. In difference to the standard approaches that stick to some particular type of memorization, we analyze different possibilities of how the value system can influence the building of the elements of the abstraction layer. First, the signal from the value system can be used for classification, (case A:S:R and A:SM:R, A:SE:R). Second, it can be used for the optimization of the motor action as a part of the abstraction (case A:SE:O). Finally, the elements can be the result of the optimization of the abstraction structure itself with respect to the cost of internal actions e.g. planning, attention, that have to be carried out on this structure (case A:A:O). We consider the first two cases and we show how the usage of one abstraction type can support the building of another abstraction type so that we can organize an incremental process improving the bootstrapping system. In the next chapter we present the implementations that validate our approach.

4 Incremental Building of Developing Systems

The following chapter presents the implementation of our proposal for bootstrapping a developing system. We start first with testing the idea of homeostatic control while keeping the representations in the abstraction layer very simple. Then we move on to increasingly complex representations following the incremental process of improvement described in Section 3.3.3.

4.1 Learning in interaction and learning to interact

In our first implementation we follow the principle of horizontal simplification. We include all three ingredients of the bootstrapping proposed in the previous chapter: an innate reactive layer, a homeostatic control of general rewards, and an abstraction layer, but we keep these ingredients simple. Our goal is a system that builds-up on its abilities by creating a favorable interaction with the environment so as to learn existing regularities, see Section 3.3.3. As an example we take here a human-robot interaction with online learning of visual object recognition. The innate behavior is not task-specific. Instead it provides a general ability to make a visual search between all interesting (regarding color, contrast, structure, etc.) locations. This ability bootstraps the interaction with environment. We define how the system can measure the quality of interaction and use these measurements as general, task-unspecific rewards. The system explores its behavior and memorizes its experience with respect to these rewards. In this way the system acquires the elements of the abstraction layer that can be used for a better control of the interaction. Figure 4.1 shows the focus of this section with respect to overall design proposal made in Chapter 3.

4.1.1 Bootstrapping system: saliency-driven gaze selection

For our experiments we use a humanoid stereo camera head (see Figure 4.3) which can move in pan and tilt direction. It is compatible with the hardware of the ASIMO robot. For ASIMO's hardware specifications please see the homepage
   http://world.honda.com/ASIMO/technology/spec.html.

The system selects its gaze direction q_T according to a saliency map S^w in the spirit of [27]. This map is a weighted sum of visual saliency S_V, disparity saliency selection S_D, and motion saliency selection S_M as illustrated by the lower part of Figure 4.2. The visual saliency computation provides a map S_V of "interesting" (regarding color, contrast, or structure) locations. The disparity saliency selection S_D computes disparities and selects the closest region within a specific distance range and angle of view. This simple mechanism represents a first

4 Incremental Building of Developing Systems

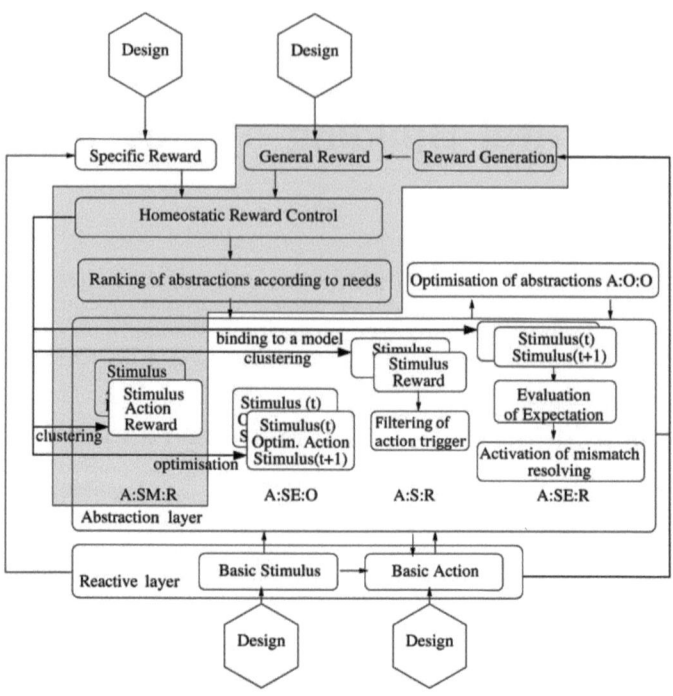

Figure 4.1: Incremental building of the bootstrapping system for open-ended development. The dark area shows the focus of this section.

approximation to the concept of the peripersonal space (see Figure 4.3). This concept allows to create shared attention between the system and the human on a very low level without any psychological concepts. The motion saliency selection produces a map S_M with an activation corresponding to the largest connected area of motion within a defined time-span. All the maps are transformed from camera coordinates (pixels) to the motor coordinates that describe the necessary pan-tilt head rotation (q_T) in order to move the pixel in the center of the left camera. All transformed maps are weighted and summed up to the final saliency map S^w (see Figure 4.2). The final map is the input to the gaze selection that uses a Dynamic Neural Field (DNF) governed by Amari equation [37, 39]. The dynamics of DNF supports a spatio-temporal integration and allows the selection to have a hysteresis.

The weights of the maps define the behavior of the system. The weights (w_V for visual saliency, w_D for disparity, and w_M for motion) are set according to the information priority (from highest to lowest): disparity, motion, visual saliency ($w_D = 3.0$, $w_M = 2.0$, $w_V = 1.0$). Without any interaction the gaze selection is autonomously driven by the visual saliency and the memory of the gaze selection. A natural way for humans to raise the attention is to step into

4.1 Learning in interaction and learning to interact

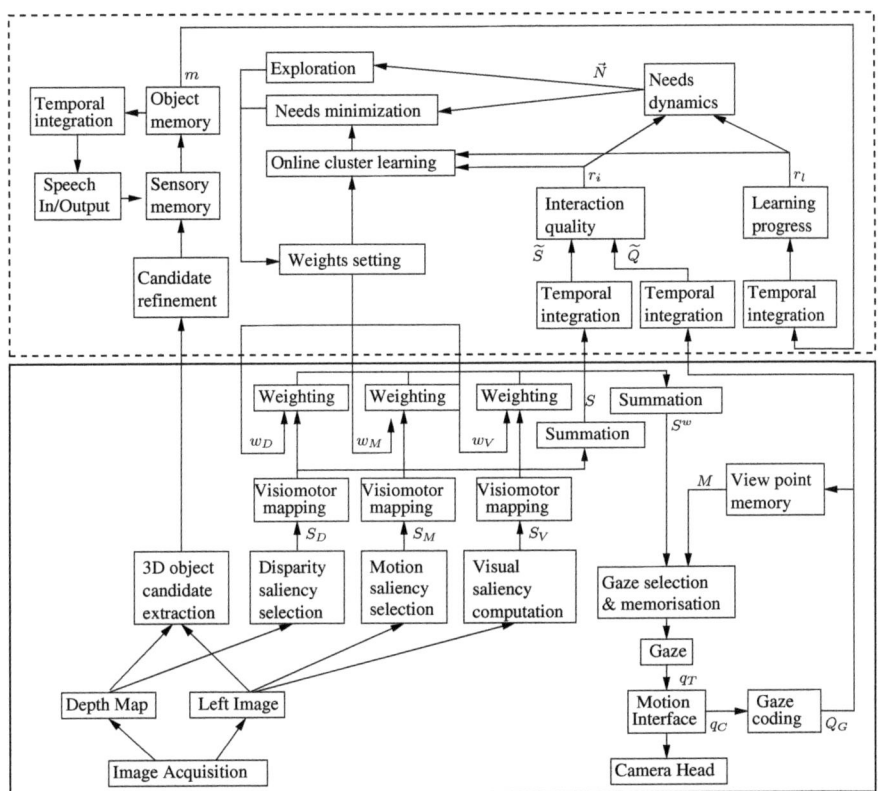

Figure 4.2: Systems schematics. The solid box shows the reactive layer that bootstraps the interaction with the environment. The dashed box shows the abstraction layer. It consists of the object recognition learning and behavior clustering and learning. See text for detailed description.

the field of view and wave at the system. Due to the chosen weights the system will immediately gaze in the direction of the detected motion. The motion cue can be used continuously in order to keep the gaze direction of the system oriented towards the hand until the hand enters the peripersonal space. Again, due to the chosen weights the signal from the peripersonal space will dominate the behavior of the system. This means that the system will continuously fixate the hand and what is in the hand of the user. Finally the object recognition learns whatever is shown to the system in this way.

4 Incremental Building of Developing Systems

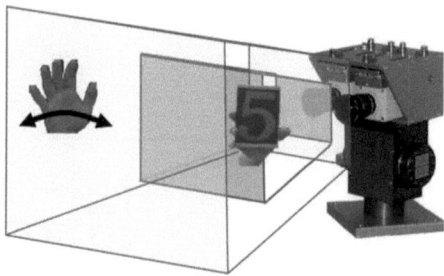

Figure 4.3: Schematic visualization of the peripersonal space approximation. The inner volume represents the peripersonal space, the outer volume the complete field of view with the sensitivity to visual and motion cues.

4.1.2 Object learning and recognition

The visual region comprising the closest "object" within the peripersonal space, described in section 4.1.1, is the candidate / hypothesis of the object to be learned or recognized. This region comprises usually the object of interest and the hand of the presenter. With a segmentation based on the adaptive scene dependent filters proposed in [20] the visual elements corresponding to the hand are removed and the segmentation of the object with respect to the background is improved. The classifier then has then to deal with the remaining visual parts not belonging to the object of interest.

Those enhanced segments are further processed by the model of the ventral visual pathway of Wersing & Körner [61] to obtain a complex feature map representation that is based on 50 shape and 3 color feature maps. The color channels are just downsampled images in the three RGB channels. The output is a high-dimensional view-based representation of the input object, that serves to classify or learn the current object. Those representations are stored within the sensory memory as long as the object did not leave the peripersonal space. This time history of sensory object hypotheses is communicated to the object memory.

Within the object memory, a persistent representation that carries consolidated and consistently labeled object views is created. As long as an object is presented within the peripersonal space and has not been labeled or confirmed, the obtained feature map representations of views are stored incrementally within the sensory memory. At the same time, all newly appearing views are being classified using the persistent object memory. If the human teacher remains silent, then the system will either generate a class hypothesis, or reject the presented object as unknown and verbalize this using the speech output module. The human teacher can confirm the hypothesis or make a new suggestion on the correct object label. As soon as feedback by the teacher is available, the learning architecture starts the concurrent transfer from the sensory memory buffer into the consolidated object memory. This extends over the whole history of collected views during the presentation phase and also proceeds with all future views, as long as the object is still present in the peripersonal space. The labeling of the current object can be done by the teacher at any time during the dialogue and is not restricted to being a reaction on a class hypothesis of the recognition system. The concept of a context-dependent memory buffer makes a separation into training and testing phases unnecessary. The transfer from the sensory to the object memory is sufficiently fast to remain unnoticed to the human trainer and the learning success can be immediately tested, allowing for a real online learning interaction.

The mechanism facilitating the online learning is an adaptive vector quantization working on the feature representations as detailed in [29]. For each class a set of reference vectors is maintained. During learning, new reference vectors are created if the incoming patterns are sufficiently different from the already stored reference vectors for this class. For recognition, the incoming patterns are efficiently compared to the reference vectors of all classes.

The speech input and output is very important for the intuitive training interaction with the system. We use a system with a headset, which is the current state-of-the-art for speaker-independent recognition. The vocabulary of object classes is specified beforehand, to be able to label arbitrary objects we also use wildcard labels such as "object one", "object two" etc.

The resulting system shows a natural and smooth interaction with users. The hypothesis built into the system is that objects are presented within the hand, otherwise there are no assumptions about the objects. The properties leading to the robust recognition are distributed over the system. Translation invariance is achieved by gazing, scale invariance by normalizing the 3D object hypothesis by distance estimation delivered by the disparity computation. Rotation invariance is enhanced by normalizing the first principle axis of the object. The online learning performance is facilitated by the efficiency of the hierarchical processing and by the locality of the plasticity, i.e. learning only on the highest hierarchy level.

For more details on the vision part the reader is referred to [60]. Here we focus on the more abstract level of elements in order to present the coupling with the behavioral part. The most significant elements here are the disparity saliency selection with the corresponding weight w_D and the object memory. The modulation of w_D determines whether the attention of the system is drawn towards the object within the peripersonal space ($w_D > 0$) or whether it is repelled by the object within the peripersonal space ($w_D < 0$). The behavior learning will build on this modulation. The object memory provides the signal for the learning progress. It is based on the number of reference vectors that are transferred from the sensory memory buffer into the consolidated object memory.

4.1.3 Extension by unspecific reward system for behavior learning

The previous section described gaze selection with fixed weights of saliency channels. Our experiments ([19],[18]) show that such an attentional system provides a natural means of interacting with a robot for learning object recognition. However it has a following drawback: if an object is not presented by a human, but is close to the system, then it will also be fixated. This can be interpreted as a symbol grounding problem. Indeed, the mapping from the depth signal to the interaction hypothesis is created by the designer. The reality does not always correspond to this mapping but the system can not find out the discrepancy on its own. It can not detect if the depth signal comes from "background" or from the user who wants to interact.

One possible solution would be the redesign of the hypothesis about the object to learn. Additionally to the closeness we could require the presence of motion, skin color or speech. There are two reasons why we prefer another solution.

First, the mentioned above percepts are not sufficiently robust. The user can present an object for a while without moving and saying anything. He can do it also in a way that the

4 Incremental Building of Developing Systems

skin is not visible. Also vice versa, it is possible that the speech, skin color and movement are present without an intention of the user to teach the system an object. The state of an object as "learnable" or not is rather hidden than perceptive.

The second, and more important reason is our aim to equip the system with means to recognize on its own the failure of the reactive behavior and to adapt appropriately. For this purpose we introduce two measures of the quality of system's behavior: the quality of the interaction with the environment and the learning progress of the object recognition.

Generally speaking, the quality of the interaction with the environment is high if the action of the robot leads to consistent sensory observations. In our example we measure directly the correlation between the gaze direction and the position of the salient object. Thus the quality of interaction is high if either the robot tracks the object, or the object follows the gaze direction of the robot. Both situations are favorable for object recognition learning. Below we describe how we measure the correlation. First, the current gaze direction q_C is represented as a gaussian blob with the center at q_C in the 2D-motor-map $Q_G(i_p, i_t)$, $i_p = [1..N_p]$, $i_t = [1..N_t]$ of possible gaze directions, where N_p, N_t are the dimensions of the discretized motor space of pan/tilt rotation of the head. This is the same representation type as the saliency map S after the visiomotor mapping and thus the two maps Q_G and S can be compared for the measurement of the correlation, (see Figure 4.2). Both non-weighted saliency map S and the gaze representation Q_G become subject to low-pass filtering in time because we want to capture not only strict synchrony between the gaze direction and the object position, but also correlations within a certain time-window. In order to estimate the degree d_c of correlation, the two low-passed maps $\tilde{S}$ and $\tilde{Q}$ are element-wise multiplied and the result is summed-up and scaled as follows:

$$d_c(t) = \frac{1}{\alpha_c} \sum_{i_p=1, i_t=1}^{N_p, N_t} \tilde{S}(t, i_p, i_t)\tilde{Q}(t, i_p, i_t),$$

where α_c is the scaling factor:

$$\alpha_c = \max \left\{ \sum_{i_p=1, i_t=1}^{N_p, N_t} \tilde{S}(t, i_p, i_t), \sum_{i_p=1, i_t=1}^{N_p, N_t} \tilde{Q}(t, i_p, i_t), 1 \right\}.$$

The correlation degree $d_c(t)$ reflects the quality of interaction only if the head is moving. To measure the intensity of the head movement we look if the changes in the gaze direction map $\tilde{Q}$ are high:

$$d_m(t) = \frac{1}{\alpha_m} \sum_{i_p=1, i_t=1}^{N_p, N_t} f_l\left(\tilde{Q}(t, i_p, i_t) - \tilde{Q}(t-1, i_p, i_t)\right),$$

where $f_l(x)$ is a linear threshold function with zero threshold:

$$f_l(x) = \begin{cases} 0, & \text{if } x \leq 0; \\ x, & \text{if } x > 0, \end{cases}$$

and α_m is again the scaling factor:

$$\alpha_m = \max \left\{ \sum_{i_p=1, i_t=1}^{N_p, N_t} \tilde{Q}(t, i_p, i_t), 1 \right\}.$$

4.1 Learning in interaction and learning to interact

To get the final measure of the interaction quality r_i we multiply the correlation degree by the movement intensity:
$$r_i(t) = d_c(t)d_m(t) \,.$$

Next we describe how we measure the learning progress. An evidence for learning of the object recognition is the transfer from the sensory memory buffer into the consolidated object memory (see Section 4.1.2). Every time this transfer occurs the learning module produces a "spike":
$$m(t) = \begin{cases} 1, \text{if memory transfer,} \\ 0, \text{else} \,. \end{cases}$$

These spikes are integrated over time in order to have a signal that reflects how often the transfer occurs:
$$r_l(t) = \tau_r r_l(t-1) + m(t) \,.$$

The relaxation constant τ_r was chosen during the experiment to fit the dynamics of the learning so that the resulting measurement r_l lies in the interval comparable to the measurement of the interaction quality ($\approx [0, 2]$).

In [42] it was proposed to use the learning progress as a measure of getting better in predicting the results of one's own behavior. Here the learning progress is not a general measure for all behaviors, but specific to the object recognition. In this way we can decouple the general evaluation of the situation as favorable for learning (captured by unspecific interaction quality measure $r_i(t)$) from the learning progress $r_l(t)$ which can be delayed, and can be specific to the implementation of the learning algorithm. Let us recall the discussion about specific and general rewards in Section 3.1. In terms of that discussion, by using a general interaction reward $r_i(t)$ we can better guide the exploration and evaluation of a large parameter space than with delayed and punctual specific reward $r_l(t)$. But we need both for the behavior generation.

In order to let the system monitor the described above rewards $\vec{R}(t) = \begin{bmatrix} r_l(t) \\ r_i(t) \end{bmatrix}$ we introduce a corresponding needs vector with two elements $\vec{N}(t) \in R^2$. The needs are satisfied if their values are close to zero. If the needs are below a chosen threshold $\vec{N}_0 > 0$ they are set to this threshold. Otherwise they change according to dynamics of the Lotka-Volterra type:
$$\tau_N d\vec{N}/dt = \vec{N}(t) .* \left(\vec{R}_0 - \vec{R}(t) \right) ,$$

where $.*$ means component-wise multiplication, τ_N is a time constant, constant vectors $\vec{R}_0 \in R^2$ characterize the speed of the need growth in absence of rewards, and $\vec{R}(t) \in R^2$ are the corresponding rewards.

If the reward is absent for a long time the need overcomes the threshold where the exploration starts. As stated previously, the character of the visual behavior is defined by the weights of the saliency maps. The most relevant weight for the interaction is the weight w_D of the depth saliency selection map, because this map represents the objects that are in the peri=personal space, see Figure 4.3. In the following we will describe how new values for w_D are explored for improving the behavior with respect to the needs. The system tries out a different weight w_D^{new} of the depth saliency selection map according to the following simple heuristic: $w_D^{new} = w_D^{old} + S_E D_E$, where D_E is the direction and S_E the strength of exploration. Exploration makes N_{hyst} steps in one direction. If in all of these steps the need continues to increase, then it changes the direction D_E and increases the strength S_E.

4 Incremental Building of Developing Systems

As the system explores negative weights w_D^{new} it starts to avoid the object in peri-personal space. Indeed, the negative values suppress the selection of the region. If the object is just "background", then it does not react to avoiding and there is nearly no correlation between the action of the system and the saliency map. If the object is shown by a user, then it is natural for the user to slightly follow the head movement of the robot in order to stay in interaction. Hence through avoiding of the object the system can differentiate between an object shown by a user and a background object. Furthermore it can force the user to provide a new view of the object or to provide a new object.

This means that for the most effective learning the systems should know that

1. the tracking provides the maximal learning progress,
2. it should stop the tracking if learning progress is missing for a long time,
3. if interaction is observed while avoiding the object, then it is probable to get a learning progress by tracking and the best strategy is to switch to tracking.

Below we describe how we implement the system with properties stated above. Point two is provided by the introduction of a monitoring mechanism. Point three is covered by our choice of the rewards because the probability of "good" tracking can be derived from the similarity of rewards in interactive tracking and avoidance. The first point requires the representation of possible rewards and careful vector quantization of the behavior-reward space.

The actual implementation of the vector quantization is very simple because we were interested more in the interplay of the different parts of the system than in the perfect working of one part. We record the disparity weight and corresponding reward into a table of possible constellations. The table has the following format: $[W_C(i), \vec{R}_C(i), C(i)], i \in [1 \ldots M]$, where M is the number of recorded constellations, W_C is a weight used for disparity saliency selection, and $\vec{R}_C$ is the vector of observed rewards. The confidence C keeps the track of how good the entry matches the observing data. It is initialized with 1.0 and its updating will be described later.

The situation at the time-step t is compared to the entries of the table according to following formulae inspired by [62]:

$$\lambda_W(i,t) = \exp(-||W_C(i) - w_D(t)||^2/\delta_W^2),$$
$$\lambda_R(i,t) = \exp(-||\vec{R}_C(i) - \vec{R}(t)||^2/\delta_R^2)),$$
$$\lambda(i,t) = \lambda_W(i,t)\lambda_R(i,t).$$

The similarity measures $\lambda_W(i,t)$ and $\lambda_R(i,t)$ are close to 1.0 if the actual constellation is close to the table entry with index i. The most similar to the actual constellation is the entry with the highest responsibility $\lambda(i,t)$. The parameters δ_W and δ_R define the responsibility radius of the recorded constellations and thus the sampling rate of recording.

Every time a highest responsibility of known constellations is lower than a threshold λ_T, a new entry is appended to the table. The confidence of the best matching entry i_{best} (with highest responsibility: $i_{best} = \arg\max_i(\lambda(i,t))$) is increased if the responsibility is over a threshold C_T and decreased otherwise:

$$C(i_{best}, t) = f(C(i_{best}, t-1) + \tau_C(\lambda(i_{best}, t) - C_T)),$$

4.1 Learning in interaction and learning to interact

where $f(x)$ is a step function, so that the confidence is truncated over 1.0 and below 0.0:

$$f(x) = \begin{cases} 0.0, & \text{if } x \leq 0; \\ 1.0, & \text{if } x > 0. \end{cases}$$

If the confidence of the best matching entry is too low, then the entry is changed to the actual constellation $(w_d(t), R(t))$.

While exploring possible constellations the system may record a very improbable situation (high learning progress while avoiding of the object). On the other side some typical situations are not always persistent. For example the tracking behavior can give a high learning progress if user shows different object views and gives no learning progress if the user does not move an object. For this reason we can not use statistical learning. We have to decide whether a constellation has to be unlearnt or whether it is only actually not possible for a short time period. For this purpose we introduce a temporary measure of a reward mismatch:

$$\vec{R}_{MM}(i,t) = \begin{cases} \vec{R}(t) - \vec{R}_C(i) + \vec{R}_T, & \text{if } i = i_{best}, \\ 0.0, & \text{else}. \end{cases}$$

This value is positive if the actual reward is higher than recorded and negative if the difference to the recorded reward exceeds the tolerance margin $\vec{R}_T$.

The reward mismatch gives an a-posteriori information about how likely a reward recorded in the best matching entry is. For a-priori decision to switch the behavior we also need an a-priori information. We suppose that constellations with similar reward to the observed one are a-priori more likely.

The similarity $\lambda_R(i,t)$ as a-priori information and the reward mismatch $\vec{R}_{MM}(i,t)$ as a-posteriori information both give us a hint if it is likely to get the reward recorded in entry i. This information is accumulated over time as likelihood $l_R(i,t)$ of getting reward recorded in entry i:

$$l_R(i,t) = \tau_l l_R(i,t-1) + (1.0 - \tau_l)(\lambda_R(i,t) + \vec{R}_{MM}(i,t)),$$

where parameter τ_l expresses the conservatism of systems belief about the actual context. This parameter together with the parameter of confidence decrease τ_C has to be chosen in the way that the switching of behavior occurs on the faster time-scale than switching of the entries in the recording table.

Finally the weight of the disparity map is selected in three steps:

1. The system monitors in which constellation it is by calculating responsibility $\lambda(i,t)$.

2. The system calculates the likelihood of recorded constellations $l(i,t)$. The constellations are possible if their likelihood is higher than a threshold l_T.

3. The system chooses the weight from the possible constellation with maximal reward for the highest need. We call the index of the chosen constellation i_{max}. If both needs are at the lowest level, the priority is given to the need of the learning progress.

In the next section we will report on the character of the achieved behavior adaptation.

4 Incremental Building of Developing Systems

4.1.4 Experimental results

Figure 4.4 shows the run of a typical experiment. The weight of the disparity channel is set initially to $w_D = 4.0$. This is a pre-designed solution as described in Section 4.1.1. The first entry made by the system into the record table corresponds to just looking around without interaction and learning. About the time-step 10 the user starts teaching a new object. The second entry put into the table reflects the fact that the system can receive a high interaction quality and learning progress during tracking. About time-step 20 the user introduces a static object. It can not be learnt because it is not labeled (see the description of the learning in Section 4.1.2). It is also not interacting, thus the system decides that it is in the situation without interaction. However the system does not know yet any other behavior than tracking and keeps fixating the static object.

With time the needs are growing over the threshold and the system starts exploration. During the exploration (time-steps $30 - 70$) the system records 3 new constellations: that it can ignore an object ($w_D = 0.0$), avoid a static object and avoid an object that tries to stay in interaction. After this exploration and learning phase the system shows a more appropriate behavior. While the user presents the object statically so that the learning progress decreases (time-steps $100 - 103$) the likelihood to get learning progress from tracking decreases. At the time-steps $114, 115$ the system switches to the avoidance mode ($w_D = -2.0$). But because the user follows it, the system switches back to tracking (time-step 116). Time-steps $180, 181$ represent a similar situation. If the user does not follow, the system remains in avoidance mode or switches to ignoring (steps $188 - 196$).

Although the typical runs of the experiment led to stable solutions, we observed also the runs where the behavior switching destablized the interaction. These were the cases where the system erroneously experienced a high learning progress while avoiding the object. As our simple clustering is based on the single observations and does not take into account the long term statistics, it can not deal with such outliers. As a result, in the runs with erroneous observation the system sticked to avoidance strategy for too long period and switched to tracking too late while the user already gave up the interaction. Nevertheless the system shows the feasibility of the chosen approach under constraint that the clustering can deal with outliers.

In this section we presented an extension of the innate reactive behavior by a homeostatic control of unspecific needs as it was proposed in Section 3.1. The needs to have an interaction with the environment and to have a learning progress forces the system to explore the parameters of its reactive layer and to progress from the reactive tracking of any close object to differentiated tracking. The system continues to track only those objects that try to gain the attention of the system. These objects are likely to be presented and named by a human and are thus good candidates for the object recognition learning. In order to differentiate the control, the system memorizes its experience with the help of a clustering of the sensorimotor space according to the reward (type A:SM:R of the formalization made in Section 3.3). The modification of the gaze selection bases on the ranking of the clusters according to the current needs of the system and the likelihood that the cluster describes the current situation.

To summarize, we presented a complete system composed of an innate reactive layer, a layer of homeostatic control, and a simple abstraction layer. The system copes with four coupled dynamics: the dynamics of changing needs, changing memory (as we use an online learning), changing behavior, and the dynamics of changing reward (as the learning progress is high for

4.1 Learning in interaction and learning to interact

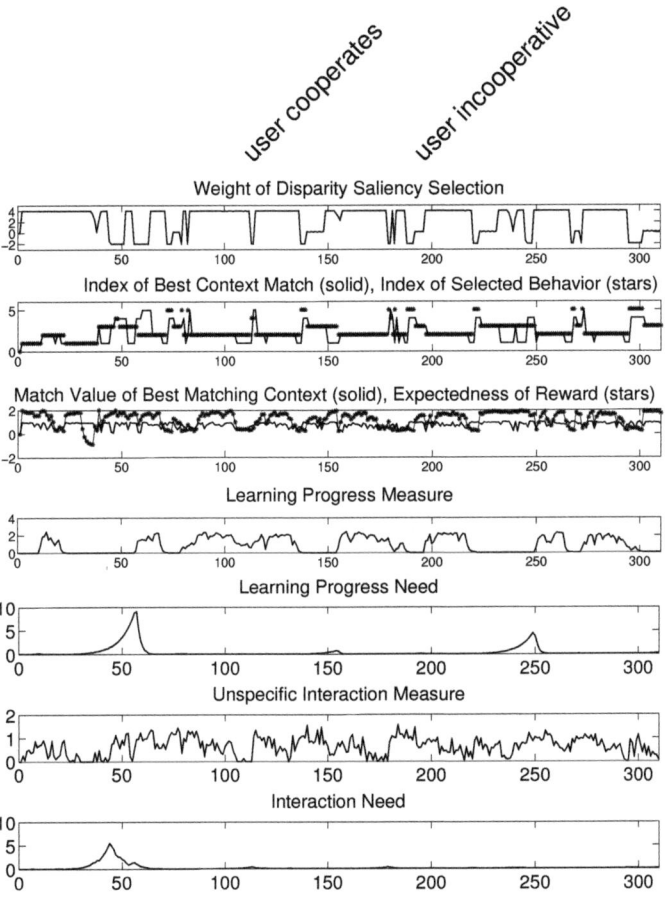

Figure 4.4: Experiment run. The upper graph shows the evolution of the disparity saliency selection weight w_D. The second graph from the top shows the index of the best matching context (i_{best}) and the index (i_{max}) of the selected weight representing the selected behavior. The third graph from the top shows the responsibility $\lambda(i_{best})$ of the best matching context and the likelihood $l(i_{max})$ of receiving reward. The fourth graph from the top shows the learning progress measure as provided from the object memory. The fifth graph from the top shows the corresponding need. The last two graphs show the unspecific interaction measure and the corresponding need. See text for more details.

4 Incremental Building of Developing Systems

a new object view and decreases afterwards). Although the typical runs of the experiment led to stable solutions, the unstable runs show that we need a stronger decoupling of different dynamics by making active use of different time scales. For example by differentiation of short-term and long-term statistics in the abstraction layer. This will be discussed in the next section.

4.2 Exploration of controllability

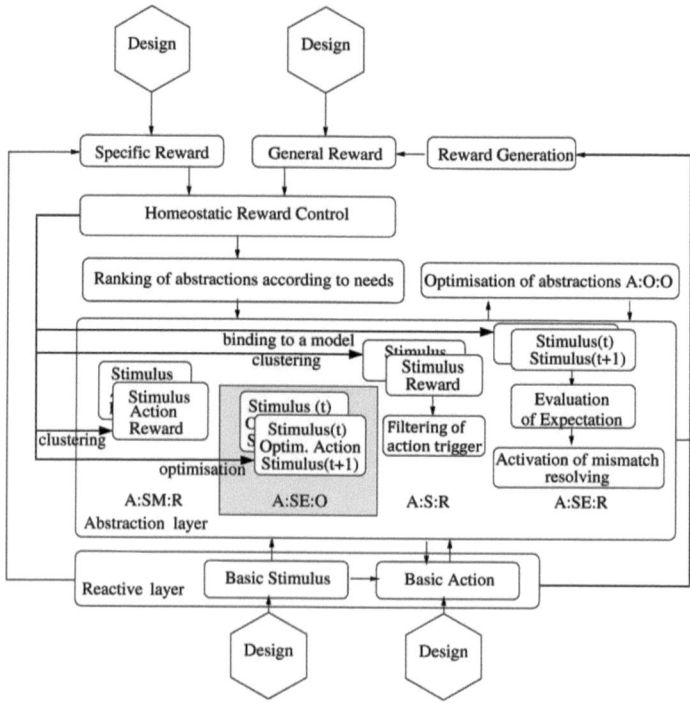

Figure 4.5: Incremental building of the bootstrapping system for open-ended development. The dark box shows the focus of this section: usage of the optimization process for acquisition and refinement of the abstractions of the type A:SE:O.

In the last section we considered the system as a whole and investigated the interplay between the dynamics of needs and the dynamics of learning, while behavior segmentation and exploration stayed very simple. Now we want to improve these aspects by monitoring the 'controllability': how reliable is the prediction of an answer to some particular behavior. Figure 4.5

4.2 Exploration of controllability

shows the focus of this section with respect to overall design proposal made in Chapter 3. We progress from the simple evaluative type of the abstraction A:SM:R used in the last section to the abstraction type A:SE:O that uses optimization of the actions and updating of corresponding expectations. The system explores its behavior and refines the abstractions so as to achieve higher controllability. We pay particular attention to the distinction between prediction errors caused by not yet learned regularities versus prediction errors caused by switching context because we aim at a system that is potentially able to learn in highly dynamical situations.

4.2.1 System instance: autonomous learning of a request gesture

A test scenario for our framework is the autonomous learning of a request gesture. There is a crucial difference between the learning of the response of an object and the learning of the response of a human. Although humans give typical responses, these responses can strongly vary depending on the hidden states of the human, such as e.g. the human's interpretation of robot's behavior. Such hidden states can be detected only after the robot executes a behavior and no reliable prediction can be done. To our knowledge, until now, the implementations that use the increasing predictability of an action response as a drive of the developmental process [41], [54] do not cover the possibility of actions with multimodal response distributions depending on hidden states of the interaction partner. However, such actions are an important part of the behavioral repertoire. They can be used to enquire those hidden states.

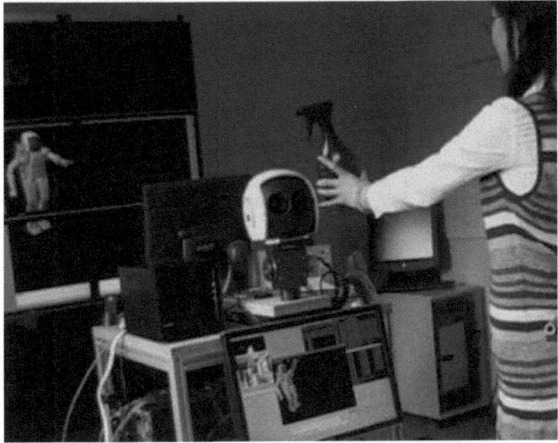

Figure 4.6: Give and show: experimental settings. The user shows an object to the camera head. The real camera moves and captures the images while the movement of the robot's hand is only simulated. The user can see the gesture displayed on a big monitor and decide how to react: give the object to the robot or only show it. The second monitor on the bottom is used to display internal states of the system for debugging purposes.

For our experiments we use a real stereo-camera head moving in pan-tilt direction together

4 Incremental Building of Developing Systems

with a simulation of the rest of the body. The stable solution can be directly transferred to the ASIMO platform thanks to the uniform software-hardware interfaces. In Figure 4.6 we show the experimental setting where the user can interact with the camera in real time while observing the simulated hand gesture on the screen bellow the head.

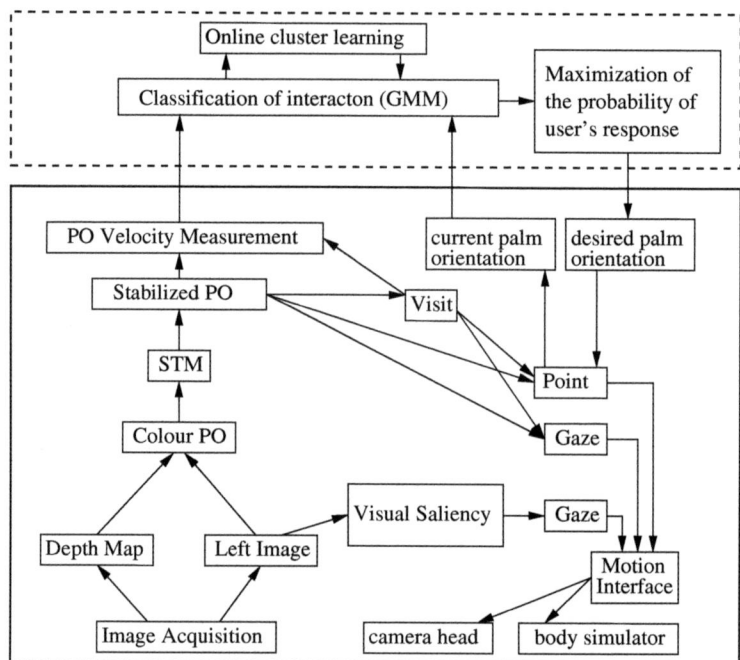

Figure 4.7: Give and show: system's graph. The solid box shows the reactive part: saliency-based gaze selection together with tracking and pointing to the object. This bootstrapping is used for refinement of the pointing by exploration of palm orientation. The monitoring of the user's reaction by means of object's velocity allows a distinction between request and show gestures. This part that builds abstractions for the refinement of the reactive behavior is shown by a dashed box. See text for more details.

In order to bootstrap the interaction with the environment we use the concept of proto-objects developed at the Honda Research Institute Europe, [9]. The proto-objects correspond to coherent regions or groups of features in the field of view that can be re-referenced over time, i.e. can be tracked. For example a proto-object can be a color blob or a blob of similar estimated depth (in the same terms as the concept of peripersonal space, see Figure 4.3). It is important not to confuse the re-referencing of a proto-object with the classification or identification of an object. The re-referencing needs only a metric in the feature space without having a precise model about what is tracked. Exactly this is the advantage of proto-objects: they can be tracked and pointed to without further model-based processing, e.g. without object recognition. This is a property we need for the bootstrapping of a task-unspecific interaction with the environment. Figure 4.7 shows the reactive bootstrapping (solid box) and the extension by parameter exploration and behavior clustering.

In the experiment the robot explores the effect of changing its palm orientation while pointing. The hand outstretched with the palm pointing upwards is typically interpreted as a request (Fig 4.9, b)). For other palm orientations the ambiguity of the user response is higher because the user can interpret even a showing gesture as a request. The response is therefore not fully predictable because it depends on the non-observable interpretation of the robot's gesture by the human. Although the response is not fully predictable, the robot should capture the fact that the hand outstretched with palm up leads to more predictable responses than other palm orientations and use preferably unambiguous gestures.

4.2.2 Segmentation of sensorimotor flow into predictive models with the help of a Gaussian Mixture Model

The robot acquires possible classes of user responses with the help of online learning of a Gaussian Mixture Model (GMM) for the joint probability distribution $p(a, r)$ of action a (palm orientation) and user response r. The user response is measured as the velocity of an object between two subsequent stops. The coordinates are chosen in such a way that if the user gives the object to the robot, then the object's velocity is positive. By choosing this way to measure the response we obviate the definition of a particular time to measure the user's reaction. The authors of [13] made an attempt to measure the user reaction at a fixed time, but they report that they encountered severe problems because the reaction time various strongly across different users. In our approach only a time-out while waiting for the reaction needs to be specified, not the specific time of measurement.

The GMM is used to make predictions and to control the palm orientation. We implicitly encoded a drive towards unambiguous action responses ("controllability") in the action selection mechanism. The action is chosen such as to have the highest probability of maintaining the current user response. The prediction of the response is done with the help of the conditional distribution $p(r|a)$ of the response r given action a. Due to the normalization factor in the conditional distribution: $p(r|a) = p(a, r) / \int p(a, r) dr$, the probability of getting the response is higher for unambiguous actions. Figure 4.8 illustrates this property on a simple example of the mixture of two Gaussians for an ambiguous action with two possible equally probable responses. A negligible difference in the centers of Gaussians in the action dimension (in this example 0.001) leads to strong shifts of the peaks in the conditional distribution, see Figure 4.8,b). Let us assume that additionally to the statistics of the observations represented by GMM there exists a small probability to observe any response to any action. This hypothesis is represented by a uniform distribution that is weighted by a small weight and added to the mixture. In this example the weight of the uniform distribution is set to 0.01. Then the shift of peaks away from the ambiguous action is less strong, see Figure 4.8,c). The higher the weight of the uniform hypothesis, the weaker the shift, see Figure 4.8,d). The action is chosen in a straightforward way as an action that maximizes the likelihood of the desired response. The exploration away from an ambiguous action is just a consequence of working with the

4 Incremental Building of Developing Systems

multimodal response distribution and the conditional probability.

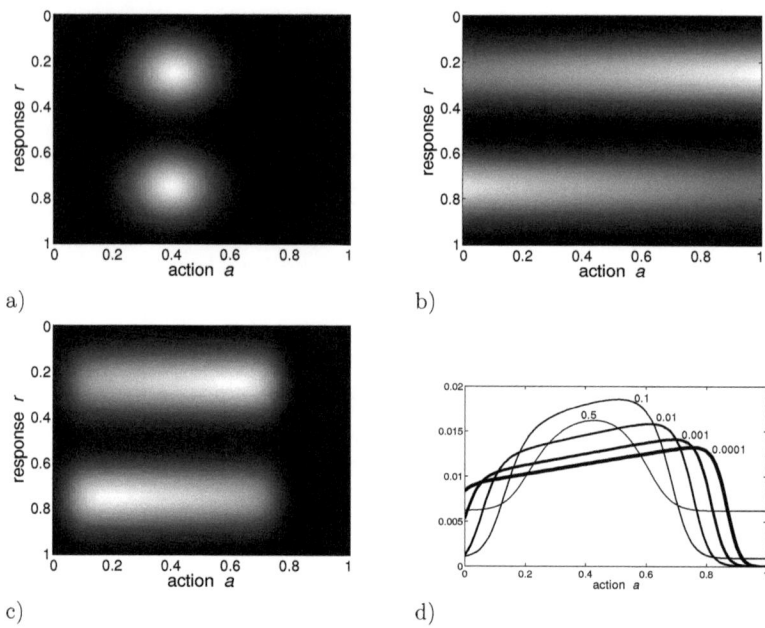

Figure 4.8: Exploration towards unambiguous actions as a consequence of usage of conditional distribution. a) An example of GMM $p(a,r)$ for ambiguous action with two possible equally probable responses. b) Conditional response distribution $p(r|a)$. The peaks in the distribution are shifted away from the ambiguous action. c) Distribution $p(r|a)$ for mixture of GMM and uniform distribution weighted by 0.01. The assumption about possible uniform action/response distribution reduces the shift of the peaks. d) Likelihood of the desired response $l(r \approx 0.2|a)$. Different lines show the likelihood for different weighting of the uniform distribution.

As we accept a multimodal response distribution, the prediction error does not lead to a change of the model if there exists a cluster that explains the observed data well. We will discuss next how we deal with the discrepancy between the a-priori prediction based on the long-term statistics and the a-posteriori classification of a current situation.

The "classical" GMM makes the assumption of observing a stationary process. The weights of the mixture describe the statistics of the cluster activations over a very long observation time. However, the activation of a cluster can be context-dependent and thus can have different statistics on a short time-scale than on a long time-scale. Therefore we need both short-term and long-term statistics for better control.

Let us denote by π_i the weights of the GMM and by $G_i(\vec{x}, \vec{\mu}_i, \mathbf{\Sigma}_i)$ the Gaussians, where $\vec{x} = \begin{bmatrix} a \\ r \end{bmatrix}$, $\vec{\mu}_i$ denote the means and $\mathbf{\Sigma}_i$ the covariance matrixes of the Gaussians, $i = 1, \ldots, N$.

4.2 Exploration of controllability

With this notations the GMM for the distribution density is

$$p(\vec{x}) = \sum_{i=1}^{N} \pi_i G_i(\vec{x}, \vec{\mu}_i, \Sigma_i).$$

Further we denote by $\hat{\pi}_i(t)$, $i = 1, \ldots, N$ the short-term statistics of the weights at the observation step t. At the initialization step we set the short-term statistics equal to the long-term statistics: $\hat{\pi}(0) = \pi_i$. With every new observation $\vec{x}(t) = \begin{bmatrix} a(t) \\ r(t) \end{bmatrix}$ we proceed first in the same way as the standard GMM approach: we calculate the a-posteriori likelihood:

$$p_i(t) = \pi_i G_i(\vec{x}(t), \vec{\mu}_i, \Sigma_i) / \sum_{i=1}^{N} \pi_i G_i(\vec{x}(t), \vec{\mu}_i, \Sigma_i), \ i = 1, \ldots, N.$$

The action executed by the system influences the statistics. In order to countermeasure this fact in the short-term statistics, we let the a-posteriori likelihood change only the weights of the mixture components that are close to the executed action. For this purpose we calculate the distance measure d_i^a:

$$\tilde{d}_i^a = \int_r G_i(\begin{bmatrix} a(t) \\ r \end{bmatrix}, \vec{\mu}_i, \Sigma_i) dr,$$

$$d_i^a = \tilde{d}_i^a / \sum_i \tilde{d}_i^a.$$

For the clusters that describe the result of the action close to executed one we have $d_i^a \approx 1.0$. The weights of these clusters in short-term statistics are shifted towards a-posteriori likelihood $p_i(t)$. The weights of others clusters are set according to the old short-term statistics $\hat{\pi}(t-1)$ and the a-priori statistics π. In sum, the short-term statistics is updated as follows:

$$\tilde{\pi}_i = d_i^a p_i(t) + (1 - d_i^a) \left[w_\pi \pi_i + (1 - w_\pi) \hat{\pi}_i(t-1) \right],$$

$$\hat{\pi}_i(t) = \tilde{\pi}_i / \sum_i \tilde{\pi}_i.$$

where the weight w_π describes how much the short-term statistics should be influenced by the long-term statistics.

The effect of filtering according to the executed action becomes clear if we consider an action with two possible responses: one described by the cluster i and another by the cluster j. Imaging that the system executes this action and observes the first of the two possible responses so that a-posteriori likelihoods $p_i(t) \approx 1.0$ and $p_j \approx 0.0$. Let us assume that yet another action, far from the executed one, is described by the cluster k, so that $p_k(t) \approx 0.0$. On the one side, in the short-term statistics we want to reflect the fact that in the current context the cluster i is much more probable than the cluster j because $p_j \approx 0.0$. On the other side, although the $p_k(t)$ is also small, the only information about the cluster k that can be used is the a-priori statistics π_k because the executed action is too far from the action described by the cluster k. Exactly this differentiation is reflected by weighting of update according to the distance to executed action: $d_i^a, d_j^a > 0$, $d_k \approx 0.0$. If we would make an update without this weighting, e.g. $\tilde{\pi}_i(t) = (1 - w_\pi) \hat{\pi}_i(t-1) + w_\pi \pi_i + p_i(t)$, then the long-term statistics would prevent the fast switching to the current context. At the same time we can not ignore

4 Incremental Building of Developing Systems

long-term statistics because we want to use the information about the response distribution of not-executed actions, like e.g. the action described by the cluster k. Those weight should not be updated to a-posteriori likelihood $p_k(t)$ that is approximately zero.

Hence, our update formulas are especially useful if the same action can have two different responses that may switch. At the same time we keep the long-term statistics about not-executed actions unchanged, so that in the choice of the next action the system can profit from both short-term and long-term statistics.

The action selection is straightforward. It takes the action that maximizes the conditional probability $p(r|a)$ of the desired response r_d using the short-term statistics $\hat{\pi}_i(t)$:

$$\begin{aligned}
\hat{p}(a,r) &= \sum_{i=1}^{N} \hat{\pi}_i(t) G_i(\begin{bmatrix} a \\ r \end{bmatrix}, \vec{\mu}_i, \Sigma_i), \\
\hat{p}(r|a) &= \hat{p}(a,r)/\int \hat{p}(a,r)dr, \\
a(t+1) &= \arg\max_a \int \exp(-||r-r_d||^2/\sigma_d^2)\hat{p}(r|a)dr,
\end{aligned} \qquad (4.1)$$

where σ_d is the variance of an exponential filter that builds a window around the desired response r_d in order to increase the reliability of the action choice.

4.2.3 Experimental results

Two experiments were conducted. In the first experiment we tested if the GMM can be learned online and can indeed capture the different ambiguities for different gestures. Instead of GMM-based action selection, the palm orientation just sampled progressively the whole possible interval from -0.5π to 0.5π independently of the current reaction of the user. In the second experiment we coupled the online learning of the GMM with the action selection described in the previous section.

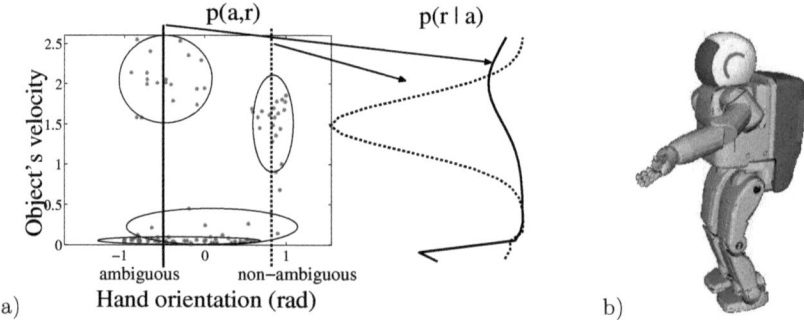

Figure 4.9: Online learning of the Gausian Mixture Module for autonomous gesture acquisition. a) The learnt action-response distribution. The solid line shows the probability of the response for the ambiguous the dashed line for the non-ambiguous gesture. b) The non-ambiguous request gesture with the palm turned up.

The online learning of a GMM in the first experiment is based on the standard expectation maximization algorithm (EM) for parameter adaptation, see e.g [7]. Following modifications

4.2 Exploration of controllability

were made in order to enable the online learning. First, not all the data is always taken for adaptation step, but only the data that considerably increases the observation likelihood if the parameter adaptation via EM is applied. Such data is accumulated in a database. The increase of the likelihood after an EM-step proved to be a better measure than the likelihood of the observation itself. The increase is a relative value and thus it allows to set a fix threshold for the decision whether to remember a new data point, e.g at thirty percent increase. In contrast, the likelihood itself depends on the current GMM and varies considerably (for more details see [65]). Second, we do not take the whole database and build always a new GMM, but we keep a current GMM until we get new 20 data points. Then these 20 new data points are used to create a new GMM with help of a standard EM algorithm with additional penalty term for a high number of components in order to prevent an over-fitting. Afterwards the old GMM and the newly created one are fused together and a final EM-step is applied on the complete database with fused GMM as initialization. Surely, this procedure does not solve the well known plasticity-stability problem that arises because the newly learnt information can erase the earlier learnt information. However, it prevents the elimination of currently not observed GMM components which would occur if we would use the standard statistical learning with EM applied to all new data. The result of online learning is presented in Fig. 4.9, a). It shows that the online learnt GMM captures indeed the lower ambiguity of the "gimme" gesture in a probability distribution.

In the second experiment we focus on the difference between long-term statistics and short-term statistics and we integrate together the learning of GMM and the GMM-based action selection described in the previous section. The action selection uses formulae 4.1. The calculations are done by discretization of the used variables in observation intervals $a \in [-0.5\pi, 0.5\pi], r \in [-0.5, 2.5]$ with discretization steps $\Delta_a = 0.1$ and $\Delta_r = 0.05$.

Fig. 4.10 shows a typical run of the experiment. The initial palm orientation is vertical: $a(0) = 0$. This is an ambiguous gesture. At the time-step 22 the system introduced a first GMM component describing the observation that the user does not give an object (object's velocity is nearly 0) if hand outstretched with palm orientation 0. At the time-step 100 the robot observes that the user gives an object. This leads to introduction of a new GMM component at this step, see Fig. 4.10, a), second column. As we described in the previous section, the aim of the action selection is to reproduce the last observation. Thus the robot chooses an action that maximizes the probability to get the object again. The previous section explained that due to the usage of conditional distribution in 4.1 the probability peaks are shifted away from ambiguous action. Indeed, the Fig. 4.10, b), second column, shows two high peaks away from 0 action. The right peak is slightly higher (as the second GMM component is centered slightly to the right of zero) and the upwards orientation of the palm is chosen as shown by the white cross.

At the step 309 the robot observes that the user sometimes does not give an object even for the palm-up gesture. The third component is added to the GMM, see Fig. 4.10, a), third column. In order to reproduce the observation of the not given object the robot choses again the vertical palm orientation.

At the time-step 514 the user changes his mind and gives an object to a robot again. This time the observation can be aposteriori explained by acquired GMM. Thus the system does not introduce a new component but only adapts the short-term statistics. This change of GMM weights $\tilde{\pi}$ leads to the selection of a new action that goes even further towards unamiguos gesture, see Fig. 4.10, b) for the step 514. The exploration of the palm orientation in steps 556

4 Incremental Building of Developing Systems

and 588 is also due to the adaptation of the short-term statistics.

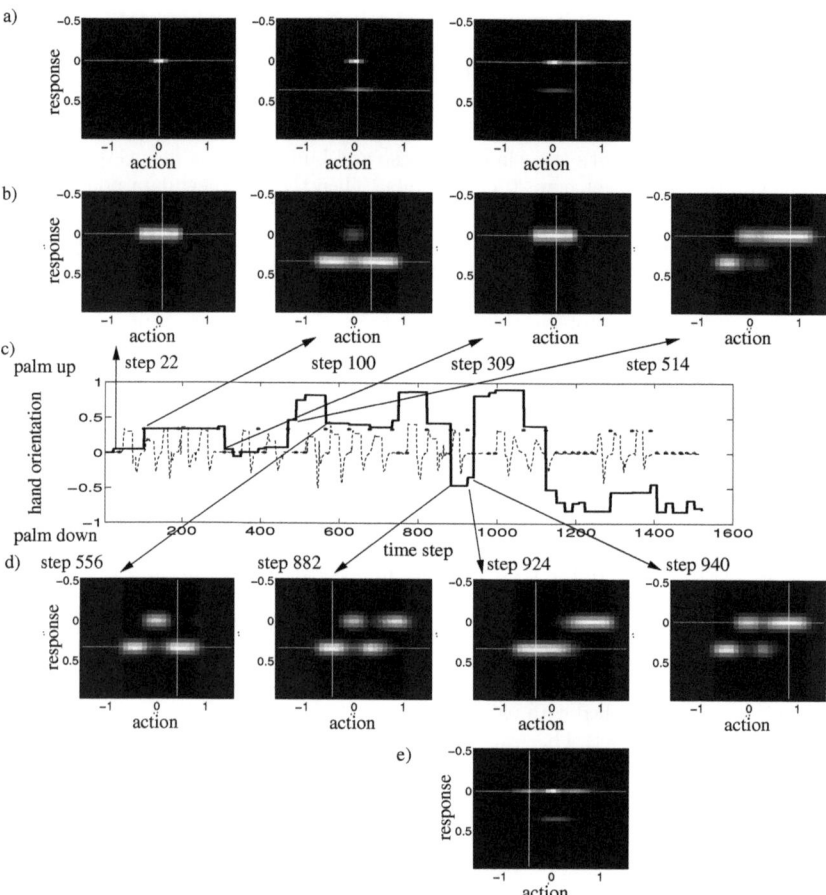

Figure 4.10: Online learning and autonomous exploration towards unambiguous gesture. The rows a) and e) show the changes in $p(a,r)$. White cross shows the center of added GMM component. The rows b) and d) show $p(r|a)$. White cross shows the selected action for desired response. c) The run of the experiment. One time-step is about 0.25 seconds. The solid line shows the chosen palm orientation. The dashed line shows the continuous object velocity. The stars show the velocity value that was taken as measurement of user's reaction, see first paragraph of Section 4.2.2. See the text for more details.

At the time-step 924 the system add a new GMM component. It describes the observation that the user does not give an object if the hand is stretched out with palm down (showing gesture). As the user changes its interpretation of the palm-down gesture and gives the object, the system immediately switches to the palm-up gesture (step 940) in order to re-experience the getting of the object. Thus the system learned to switch the context estimation with help of the sort-term statistics and to use less ambiguous gestures instead of initial vertical palm orientation.

In the future, a prediction error on the level of GMM weights estimation (difference between the a-priori and a-posteriori GMM weights) can be used for the learning on higher abstraction levels (in similar terms as described by [62]). For example one could formalize the problem by assuming that the weights are the hidden states of a Dynamic Bayesian Net. Then the system may learn the correlation of short-term statistics of the weights to observable variables. These could be the user's speech that indicates the interpretation of a gesture or a decision not to give an object, as well as observable properties of the objects that can or cannot be given. If the system learns this correlation, then it can switch faster between states. Without additional evidence for a state switch we need a certain time for the accumulation of the a-posteriori statistics in the short-term statistics in order to prevent an undesired reaction to outliers.

4.2.4 Conclusions

The presented work stresses the necessity of differentiated dealing with prediction errors. On the one hand, these errors can mean that the system has to change the model on the level of the observed data. On the other hand, they may be indicators for the need of differentiation and learning on a higher abstraction level. Finally, for some types of interaction with the environment prediction errors may be not avoidable, e.g. in interaction with a human. In these cases it may be more appropriate to use a multimodal response distribution and an a-posteriori response differentiation as a source of information for further acting. Therefore, the developmental drive is not to make no prediction errors but to make informative errors while keeping the cost of error making as small as possible. The progress of the system may be expressed by a better choice of how to acquire the information about the hidden states. "Better" can mean less energy consuming and more informative. For example, in our scenario, the system should adapt its action from a fully outstretched hand towards a more relaxed gesture accompanied by speech.

More complex hypothesis testing requires a more advanced representation and usage of expectations. The expectations should not be coupled one-to-one with the actions as it is the case for the abstraction type A:SE:O used in this section. In the next section we move on to the abstraction type A:SE:R that paves the way for implementing more elaborate hypothesis testing.

4.3 Expectation generation: beyond reactivity

In the previous two sections the building blocks of the abstraction layer contained an explicit action representation. Next, following the Section 3.3.3, we implement an indirect coupling of the abstract concepts to the control by using the generation of expectations. The goal is to extend the reactive layer by an abstraction layer so as to pave the way towards hypothesis

4 Incremental Building of Developing Systems

testing, semantic learning, and grounding. Figure 4.11 shows the focus of this section with respect to the overall design proposal made in Chapter 3.

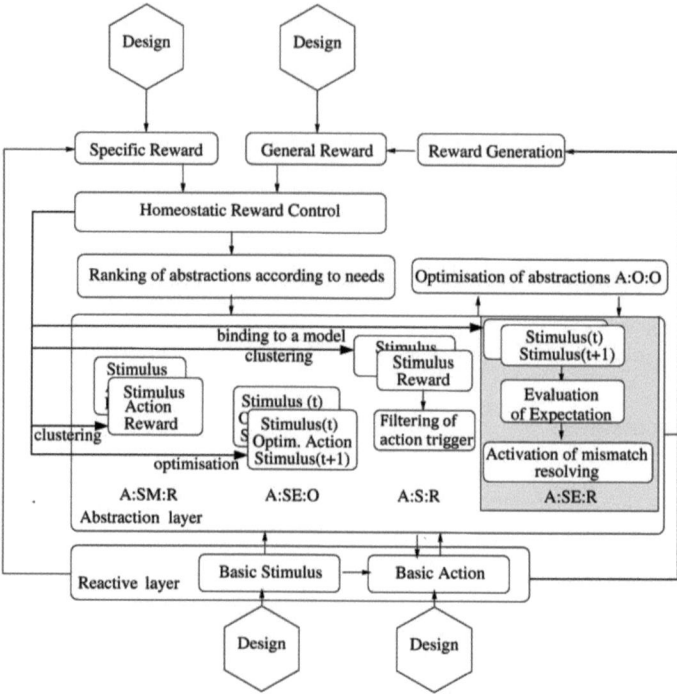

Figure 4.11: Incremental building of the bootstrapping system for open-ended development. The dark box show the focus of this section: expectation-based representation that allows a qualitative change from stimulus-driven to expectation-driven behavior.

In Section 3.3 we argued in general terms that the system observes the causalities that can be used for the memorization of the value function (abstraction of the type A:SE:R). In this section we call the models for representation of causalities a 'mental concept'. We say that the system learns a concept if it can bind different behaviorally relevant features into one expectation model $E(S)$. We recall that we see the abstraction layer as a part of the control system that insures an explicit reward monitoring. In this context we use the expression 'concept' not in the sense of a passive world model, but as a potential trigger of an expectation-driven behavior.

It is crucial to keep concepts embedded in the behavior. The system should not passively 'perceive' but actively evaluate and refine/relearn the concepts. We turn our reactive system into an active system by the generation of expectations. One part of the bound to a concept features generates expectation for the rest. These expectations are compared to the current features. If the difference is high, the mismatch triggers a behavior that can potentially resolve

4.3 Expectation generation: beyond reactivity

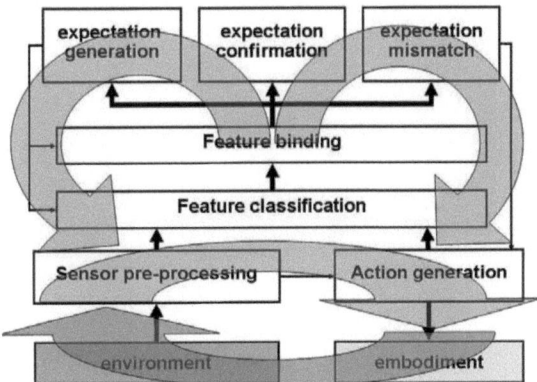

Figure 4.12: Coupling of mental concepts to a reactive layer. The loop on the lower part shows the reactive layer. The upper part generates and evaluates expectations with the help of an associative memory. In this upper part two loops are active: to the left the loop of expectation-based perception and to the right the loop of expectation-based action.

the conflict as described in Section 3.3.3. This process brings the system back into the situation where it learned the binding to the concept, so that the system can check its correctness. In this way our system achieves a tight coupling between sensing and acting not only on the reactive level but also on the level of expectations generated by mental concepts (see Figure 4.12).

4.3.1 Experimental setup and system architecture

One possible instantiation of our architecture is a system that generates expectations by using associations of speech labels to behaviorally relevant non-speech feature classes. For example the system learns that humans use the word 'table' for flat surfaces at the height of their waist. This is behaviorally relevant, because the naming of the 'right thing' with a 'right word' can trigger a primary social reward at the early stage of development and serve as a sub-goal in later stages (e.g. asking for the table if you need to deposit something). We want to emphasize that we do not reduce the learning of concepts to the learning of words. We consider the binding of a word to behaviorally relevant non-speech features as one possible scenario for learning mental concepts.

We implement our system on the humanoid robot ASIMO equipped with stereo vision cameras. The auditory signal for audio saliency is recorded by microphones mounted on ASIMO. The auditory signal for the speech recognition is recorded via a headset used by a human. Figure 4.13 shows the experimental setup while Figure 4.14 shows the overall system design.

59

4 Incremental Building of Developing Systems

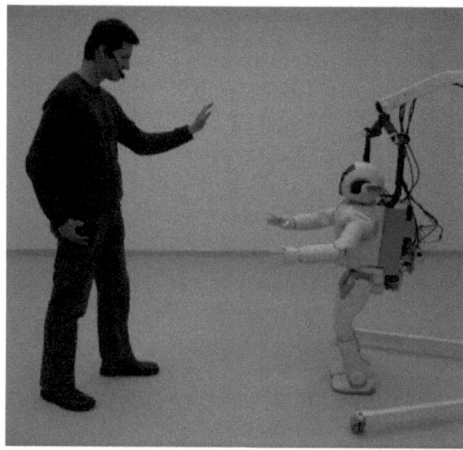

Figure 4.13: Experimental setup. The humanoid robot ASIMO interacts with a user in a reactive way by approaching and reaching for a proto-object. The user wears a headset for recording the speech signal. The user can teach the robot speech labels which describe behavior-relevant features of interaction: properties of proto-objects or the activity of the robot.

Reactive layer

We build our system incrementally: for the bootstrapping we re-use the mechanisms introduced in the last two sections: the saliency-driven gaze selection and the tracking and pointing at the proto-objects. These two control loops build the reactive layer. They run in parallel and the priority in conflict resolution is given to the target generated by the proto-objects. Thus, while there is no proto-object the system is driven by saliency and it switches to pro-object tracking whenever proto-object appears. The proto-object generation is enhanced in two directions. First, apart of the depth-based and color-based proto-objects the system can now generate proto-objects for a blob of coherent motion and a blob of coplanar 3D-points. Second, the blobs of different origins can be merged according to their 3D-position.

The tracking and pointing uses the whole body motion [17]. The walking is incorporated into the whole body control and need not to be addressed separately. During tracking and pointing the robot at the same time adjusts the distance to the proto-object to its preferred 'comfortable' distance. We emphasize that these reactive behaviors are applicable to all proto-objects and create thus a general ability to interact with environment.

Several behaviors can be active at the same time. The basic behaviors implemented are: approaching the proto-object and returning to the initial position, pointing at proto-object with left or right hand, as well as a number of gestures: nodding the head as a 'Yes', shaking the head as a 'No', raising up the left or right hand as to show that the system is learning. The selection of behaviors is done by a competitive selection mechanism (arbiter) in form of a non-linear dynamical system [4, 9]. The state of the arbiter, i.e. the result of the competitive

4.3 Expectation generation: beyond reactivity

selection, at any time can be described by the vector $\vec{a}$ of current behavior activation values. This vector can be either stored to bias the reactive layer later on or be mapped bidirectionally to action classes such as 'forward' and 'return'.

If no top-down input is present (purely reactive case) the behavior selection is solely based on a fitness value F_i that is provided by each behavior. Top-down input - in our case from the expectation generation system - can act as an additional bias β_i to the fitness of each behavior so that the competitive advantage C_i provided as input to the selection mechanism is a sum $C_i = F_i + \beta_i$. This serves as both a way to trigger certain gestures - nod head, shake head, learning gesture - and a way to push the reactive layer in the direction of a memorized behavior activation state.

Since this external influence to the reactive layer always acts merely as a bias, the reactive system is still fully functional with respect to non-biased interaction behaviors while under the influence of top-down input. Practically this means that ASIMO will e.g. still fixate and reach for objects when a 'return' command was issued and ASIMO is thus walking backwards.

Extension by an abstraction layer

While a proto-object is stably tracked by the reactive layer, the system extracts the features of the proto-object, the state of the behavior activation, and the speech features. In order to stabilize the learning we suppose that all non-speech features can be reliably classified. That means they have already been acquired in earlier developmental stages - e.g. the classification of flat surfaces as relevant for depositing behavior - or are predesigned - so to speak genetically encoded. We use a mask that we call 'evaluation mask' $\vec{\mathcal{E}}$ for differentiating between reliable, pre-designed channels and channels to learn. This mask filters the input to the associative memory in such a way that data from a learning channel requests a confirmation, whereas the data from reliable channels sends a confirmation that it can be used as a teaching signal. This mechanism will be explained in more detail in the next section.

An attention mechanism further restricts the channels that can generate teaching signals. In our framework attention is implemented in form of expectation for some particular feature channel. This expectation is raised by specific, predesigned user utterances that we call 'learning criteria'. For example if the user says 'learn where this object is', an expectation of activity for any class in the position classifier is generated. Obviously a predesigned link from a known 'learning criterion' utterance to the channel expectation is a strong simplification. Still, this link is nothing but an association and thus it could be learned as well.

The fact that humans use words to name the features is also known to the system and is represented by a predesigned association matrix of the associative memory. It contains a non-zero element at location (i, j) if the feature classes (i) and (j) are associated. In contrast to detailed correlation, associations represent the general information that the features can be bound together. Using this associative memory the system can generate a teaching signal and learn the speech classes. The details of speech processing and learning of the new labels are not the focus of this work and can be found in [11].

We use online learning, thus the learnt classes can immediately be evaluated. By using the associative memory again the speech channel now generates expectations for non-speech-features. For example when the human says 'table' the system expects to see a flat surface at the height of the waist. If the currently tracked object does not have the expected features then

4 Incremental Building of Developing Systems

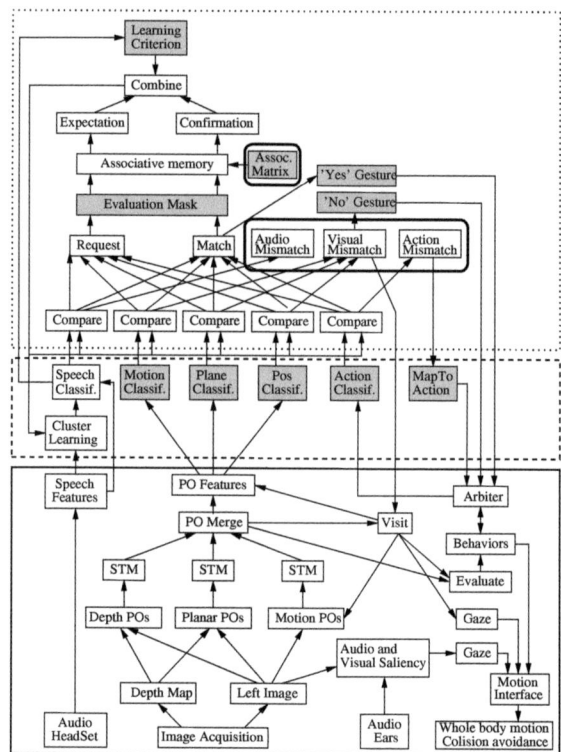

Figure 4.14: Incremental system design. The solid box on the bottom shows the implementation of the reactive part that comprises saliency-driven gazing and tracking/reaching for proto-objects. The dashed box displays the layer of feature classification. The dotted box shows the abstraction layer of expectation generation based on the associative memory.

the expectation mismatch inhibits the reactive tracking of this object. The system switches to the tracking of another object until the expected object properties are seen or a time-out cancels the expectation. The expectation mismatch in the description of the action executed by the system can directly activate the respective actions via a bias $\vec{\beta}$ to the competitive behavior selection mechanism described on page 61. Thus the system can be taught 'command'-like utterances that influence the action of the system without disabling the autonomy. As soon as expectations are met or the time-out withdraws the expectations, the system continues to interact with its environment in a reactive manner.

In order to make the behavior of the system understandable for the user, the robot communicates the state of the expectation. In case of an expectation mismatch it shakes its head ('No'

4.3 Expectation generation: beyond reactivity

gesture) and in case of a match it nods ('Yes' gesture). The gestures are triggered via a bias vector $\vec{\beta}$ in a way similar to the associated 'commands'. In the future we will extend the system by means to monitor the human reaction to the Yes/No gestures. Then the active evaluation of the expectation can be used for the refinement or relearning of the corresponding concept.

The generation of the proto-objects, the extraction and classification of the visual features as well as online learning of speech clustering are not the subject of this work. These parts were implemented by our colleagues and are described in more details elsewhere [11], [52]. Focus of this work is a general system design that allows the extension of the reactive system by expectation generation and evaluation.

4.3.2 Expectation generation and evaluation

In this section we discuss the details of the expectation generation and evaluation that takes place in the bottom-up/top-down loop via the associative memory (see Figure 4.12).

As we already mentioned, all feature classifiers are treated in the same way. Let us denote by c the index of the feature channel, by X_c the feature, and by F_c the classifier. The output of every classifier at time-step t_c is a vector of values $F_c^i(X_c)$ that represent the likelihood that X_c belongs to a class i. We consider the time-step as being specific for the classifier because all classifiers are running in parallel and thus have different rates. For motion the F_c^i are binary values: 1.0 if the proto-object is generated from a motion channel and 0.0 otherwise. For plane and position classification we use a population code: $F_c^i = d(X_c, X_c^i)$, where X_c^i is the center of the i-th cluster and $d(x, y)$ is a metric, e.g. $d(x, y) = \lambda \exp(-\frac{\|x-y\|^2}{\sigma^2})$. Every classifier output is the bottom-up input $\vec{I}_c^{bu}(t_c)$ to a module which we call 'compare' (see Figure 4.14). The second input $\vec{I}_c^{td}(t_c)$ to this module is a top-down expectation generated via the associative memory. The bottom-up feature classification is compared to the expectation. The 'compare' module has three outputs: 'request' $\vec{H}_c^R(t_c)$, 'match' $\vec{H}_c^Y(t_c)$, and 'mismatch' $\vec{H}_c^N(t_c)$. Figure 4.15 shows the internal logic of the compare module described below.

If the expectations for the particular feature are negligibly small and the bottom-up input was not yet confirmed by the expectation so that the internal state is negligibly small as well, the compare module sends the 'request' output, see case a) on the top of Figure 4.15.

If both the current feature classification and the expectation are sufficiently large, then they are compared. For this purpose we calulated an overlap between the two vectors as a vector $\vec{\gamma}$, wich is an elementwise product of the positive elements of the expectation $\vec{I}_c^{td}(t_c)$ and the classification $\vec{I}_c^{bu}(t_c)$:

$$\vec{\gamma} = f_l\left(\vec{I}_c^{td}(t_c)\right) . * f_l\left(\vec{I}_c^{bu}(t_c)\right),$$

where $f_l(x)$ is a linear threshold function with zero threshold:

$$f_l(x) = \begin{cases} 0, & \text{if } x \leq 0; \\ x, & \text{if } x > 0. \end{cases}$$

The elements of $\vec{\gamma}$ are positive, thus the sum of these elements (i.e. the scalar product of expectation and classification) can be taken as a measure of the overlap. Hence, the distance between the expectation $\vec{I}_c^{td}(t_c)$ and the classification $\vec{I}_c^{bu}(t_c)$ can be defined as the inverse of a

4 Incremental Building of Developing Systems

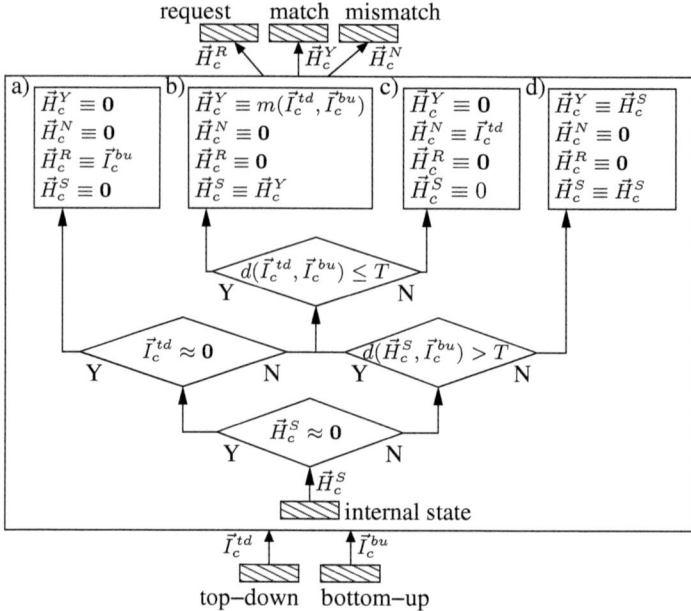

Figure 4.15: Comparison of the bottom-up classification with the top-down expectation. See the text for more details.

scalar product:
$$d(\vec{I}_c^{td}(t_c), \vec{I}_c^{bu}(t_c)) = \frac{1}{\left(f_l\left(\vec{I}_c^{td}(t_c)\right), f_l\left(\vec{I}_c^{bu}(t_c)\right)\right)}.$$

If there is no overlap between the two vectors, then the distance d is infinitely large. If this distance is smaller than a chosen threshold T, then we say that the expectation confirms the bottom-up classification. The result of the comparison $m(I_c^{td}(t_c), I_c^{bu}(t_c))$ is the overlap vector $\vec{\gamma}$ scaled by scalar product:

$$m(\vec{I}_c^{td}(t_c), \vec{I}_c^{bu}(t_c)) = \frac{f_l\left(\vec{I}_c^{td}(t_c)\right) \cdot * f_l\left(\vec{I}_c^{bu}(t_c)\right)}{\left(f_l\left(\vec{I}_c^{td}(t_c)\right), f_l\left(\vec{I}_c^{bu}(t_c)\right)\right)}.$$

This result is memorized as the internal state $\vec{H}_c^S(t_c)$ of the compare module and is propagated to its output 'match'. The request and mismatch outputs are set to zero, see case b) on the top of Figure 4.15.

If the classification contradicts the expectation, the module resets its internal state and sends the output 'mismatch', see case c) on the top of Figure 4.15.

If the bottom-up classification was already confirmed by top-down expectation and saved in

4.3 Expectation generation: beyond reactivity

internal state and the bottom-up classification did not considerably changed since that time, then the internal state and match are kept the same, see case d) on the top of Figure 4.15.

Processing of the 'mismatch' output is feature-specific. In contrast, the processing of the 'match' and 'request' outputs is not feature specific. The outputs of all channels are concatenated to a common 'match' $\vec{H}^Y(t)$ and a common 'request' $\vec{H}^R(t)$. These two vectors are multiplied component-wise with the evaluation mask $\vec{\mathcal{E}}$ that defines which channel should send a request and which channel a confirmation. In our application the speech is the channel with low confidence of the bottom-up classification that needs a confirmation, thus the elements of evaluation mask are one for speech channel and zero for entries that correspond to non-speech channels. As a result of masking operation we have masked request and masked confirmation: $\vec{\mathcal{E}}^R(t) = \vec{\mathcal{E}}.*\vec{H}^R(t)$, $\vec{\mathcal{E}}^Y(t) = (\vec{I} - \vec{\mathcal{E}}).*\vec{H}^Y(t)$, where $\vec{I}$ is a vector with all elements equal one. The associations $\vec{E}^f$ and $\vec{E}^i$ to these vectors are generated by multiplication with the association matrix $\mathbf{A}$: $\vec{E}^f(t) = \mathbf{A}\vec{\mathcal{E}}^Y(t)$ and $\vec{E}^i(t) = \mathbf{A}\vec{\mathcal{E}}^R(t)$. Here we use the notation t for time-steps. This notation is different from classifier-specific notation t_c because the operations after the concatenation run at their own rate, constrained only by the time needed to execute these operations. We do not need to synchronize the vectors that are concatenated because the processing speed is sufficiently high to react in time to all the changes.

We recall that the 'match' vector contains the features that were expected. Thus the association $\vec{E}^f$ to this vector serves as a confirmation to not yet expected features. In terms of predictive models this is a 'forward model', while the association $\vec{E}^i$ to the 'request' is analog to an 'inverse model'. It shows which features can generate the confirmation for a request. These two output vectors of the associative memory are combined with the expectation $\vec{E}^l$ generated by the attention system (learning criterion) and sent back through the loop as an expectation vector $\vec{E}(t) = \vec{E}^f(t) + \vec{E}^i(t) + \vec{E}^l(t)$. This vector is then split according to the used feature channel c (we denote this operation by $[\,]_c$) and every 'compare' module receives its corresponding part as top-down expectation $\vec{I}_c^{td}(t_c + \delta t_c) = [[\vec{E}(t)]_c](t_c + \delta t_c)$. Here we use the notation $[\,](t_c + \delta t_c)$ to stress the fact that every channel can process its top-down input with its specific rate. This splitting step closes the loop of expectation-based perception. In Figure 4.16 we schematically unfold an example of 3 successive steps of the loop in the case of an expectation match. White spaces of request and match vectors show which parts are inhibited by the evaluation mask.

Step 1. In absence of the speech signal there exist no expectations because in our experiment we assume that the non-speech channels alone are not confident enough to generate expectations. (This can be changed by setting the evaluation mask to allow also the propagation of the requests from the non-speech channels.) We start our loop monitoring at the moment when a new word was pronounced. As there is no speech expectation, the compare module propagates the bottom-up speech classification to the 'request' output. Using the associative memory this request induces the expectation of non-speech features that correspond to the speech ('inverse model').

Step 2. The 'compare' module at the non-speech side receives at the input a top-down expectation. We suppose that the word matches the perceived situation and the non-speech bottom-up classification is confirmed by the top-down input. It is memorized in an internal state of the compare module and communicated as a 'match'. With the help of the associative memory the 'match' output generates the top-down expectation for the speech ('forward model').

Step 3. Now the top-down expectation for the speech serves as a confirmation of the bottom-

4 Incremental Building of Developing Systems

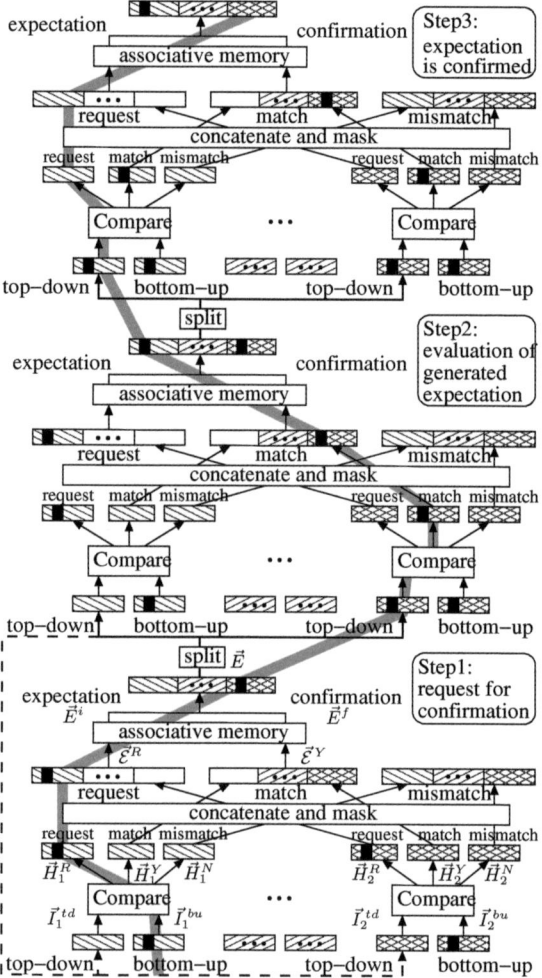

Figure 4.16: Unfolded example of 3 successive steps of the expectation generation and evaluation loop (the case of expectation match). The dashed line shows the feedback pathway if not unfolded. The grey line in the background shows the progress of changes through the loop.

up classification. Thus the speech-'compare' module accepts the bottom-up classification and transfers it to the 'match' output. The recurrent processing in the loop is converged to the state

4.3 Expectation generation: beyond reactivity

where 1) there is no activity in the request vector, and 2) both speech and non-speech bottom-up activities were confirmed and stay now in the 'match' vector until either the bottom-up input or top-down input to comparing modules considerably changes. The top-down expectation contains only the expectation for the speech as this is the classifier that is considered in our example as not sufficiently confident.

Organization of the learning

Next we would like to shed the light on the organization of the learning. As we already mentioned, in this example the system learns only on the level of feature classifiers. The associative memory represented by a correlation matrix does not change. This ensures the stability of the learning that we need for our first steps. We fix the association matrix $\mathbf{A}$ as a symmetric matrix of dimension that doubles the number N_{ns} of non-speech clusters and has a positive entry at the main and $(N_{ns} + 1)$-th diagonal:

$$\mathbf{A} = N_{ns} \overbrace{\left[\begin{array}{cc|cc} 1 & 0 & 1 & 0 \\ & \ddots & & \ddots \\ 0 & 1 & 0 & 1 \\ \hline 1 & 0 & 1 & 0 \\ & \ddots & & \ddots \\ 0 & 1 & 0 & 1 \end{array}\right]}^{N_{ns}}.$$

This matrix simply encodes the fact that there exist speech labels for non-speech clusters. Using this correlation matrix we can send a teaching signal for learning the speech clusters. The learning session is naturally integrated into the expectation generation loop with the help of two mechanisms.

The first mechanism is the 'learning criterion' signal (see Figure 4.14). This is a pre-designed user utterance that can be recognized from the beginning by the speech classifier and that specifies which classification channel will be named next by the user. For example if the user says 'learn where this object is' the learning criterion generates the expectation of activity for any class in the position classifier. Supplied with such a global expectation the 'compare' module for the position channel accepts any bottom-up input and propagates it to the 'match' output, see Figure 4.17. This output is processed then by the associative memory. We recall that the correlation matrix is organized in such a way that every class of the non-speech classifier is associated to one class on the speech side. Thus the association can be used directly as a teaching signal for speech clustering. Obviously the predesigned link from the known 'learning criterion' utterance to the modality expectation is a strong simplification. Still, this link has the same format of 'word'-feature association used in the rest of the system and potentially it could be learned as well. We emphasize that we do not use an extra system for generating a teaching signal, but use directly the expectation generation system. This design allows for further progress towards autonomous generation of the teaching signal.

The second mechanism for the integration of the learning is the confidence of the output of the classifier. As soon as a learning criterion is perceived, the system sets the confidence of the bottom-up input from the speech classifier to a small value so that the 'compare' module of

4 Incremental Building of Developing Systems

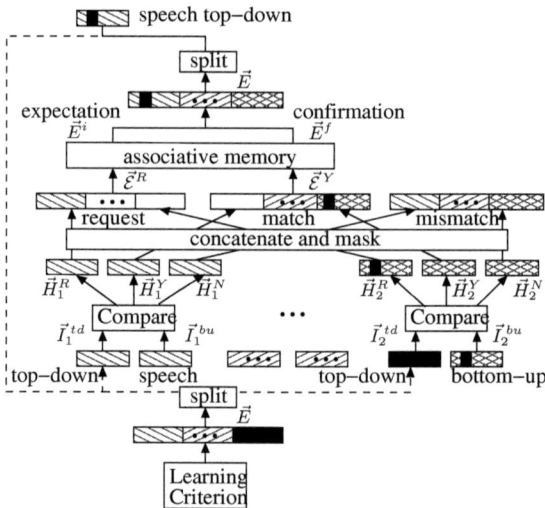

Figure 4.17: Generation of the teaching signal for the online-speech learning. At the bottom the expectation in one feature channel (e.g. position) is generated from specific utterance (e.g 'learn where this object is'). This top-down expectation propagates through the loop in the standard way (see Figure 4.16) and generates the teaching signal for the speech shown on the top.

the speech channel does not generate any expectations others than the expectation generated by the learning criterion.

4.3.3 Experimental results

Figures 4.18 and 4.19 show a run of the experiment. In this experiment, the system learns the speech clusters for labels 'left', 'right', 'table', 'chair', 'moving', 'still', 'approach' and 'return'. The text in the image shows the word learning sessions, the text on the top - the utterances for evaluation. The upper two plots display the proto object information. The labels stand for the source of proto object: 'D'- Depth, 'M'- Motion, 'P'- Plane; dark color shows high values. The second plot displays the object's position in the cylindric coordinates centered at robot's torso (waist): thick line shows the angle (rad), the dashed line - the hight, and the thin line - the depth. The plot on the very bottom shows the state of the behavior activations: 'Y'-node,'N'-shake, 'LL','LR'-learning gestures with left/right hand, 'PL','PR'-pointing with left/right hand, 'R'-return, 'A'-approach. The behaviors can run in parallel. Note the switch of the right and left hand doing pointing and learning gesture at 39 sec as the object moves from left to right. The middle 3 plots shows the state of the abstraction system. The first 9 values of expectation-, request-, and evaluation-vectors correspond to speech channel. The dashed boxes show the expectations in non-speech channels generated by learning criteria. The

4.3 Expectation generation: beyond reactivity

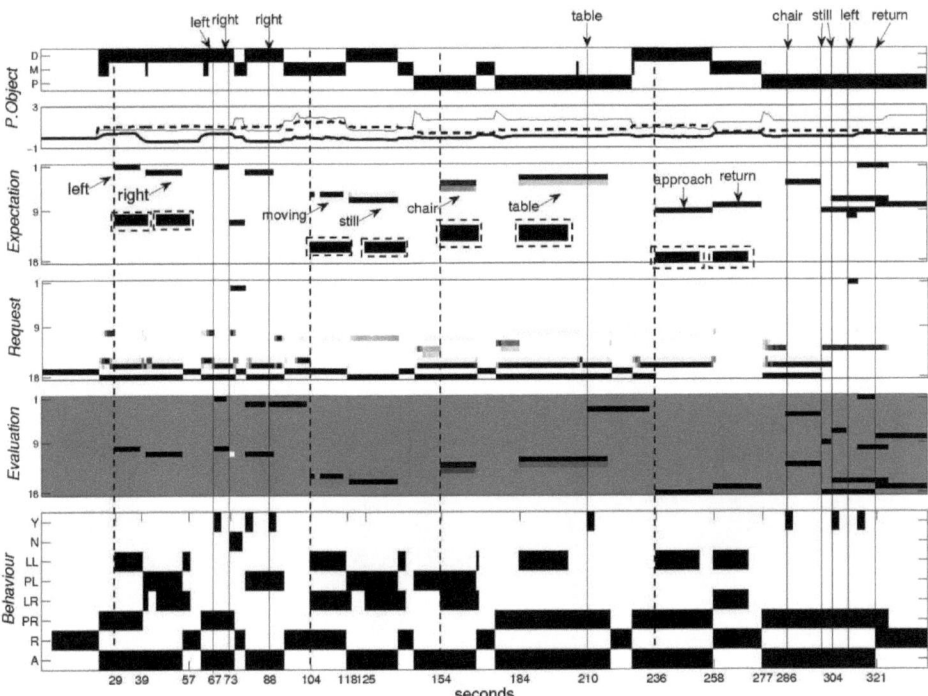

Figure 4.18: One run of the experiment: speech learning and evaluation. See the text for more details.

corresponding expectations in speech channel is used as a teaching signal. The evaluation show both the expectation match (dark) and mismatch (bright).

A typical learning session looks like follows (29-57 sec. in Figure 4.18): the user says 'learn where this object is!' (learn criteria) and then says 'left' a few times while presenting the object on the left side of the robot. If the user does not speak for 4 seconds the learning session is considered to be over. Newly learnt clusters can be immediately evaluated: The user presents an object on the left side of the robot and says 'left' (67 sec.). Speech class 'left' now raises an expectation for the interaction on the left. This expectation is satisfied here since an object is shown on the left side, so the robot nods (Yes). In contrast, when the user presents an object on the left side but says 'right' (73 sec.), this creates a mismatch (white spot in Evaluation) that triggers head shaking (label 'N' in behavior activation plot) and stops tracking. The request stays active until the robot finds the object on the right (81 sec) and nods (label 'Y').At the end of the experiment we evaluate some of the learnt labels while ASIMO is tracking a not yet seen object.

4 Incremental Building of Developing Systems

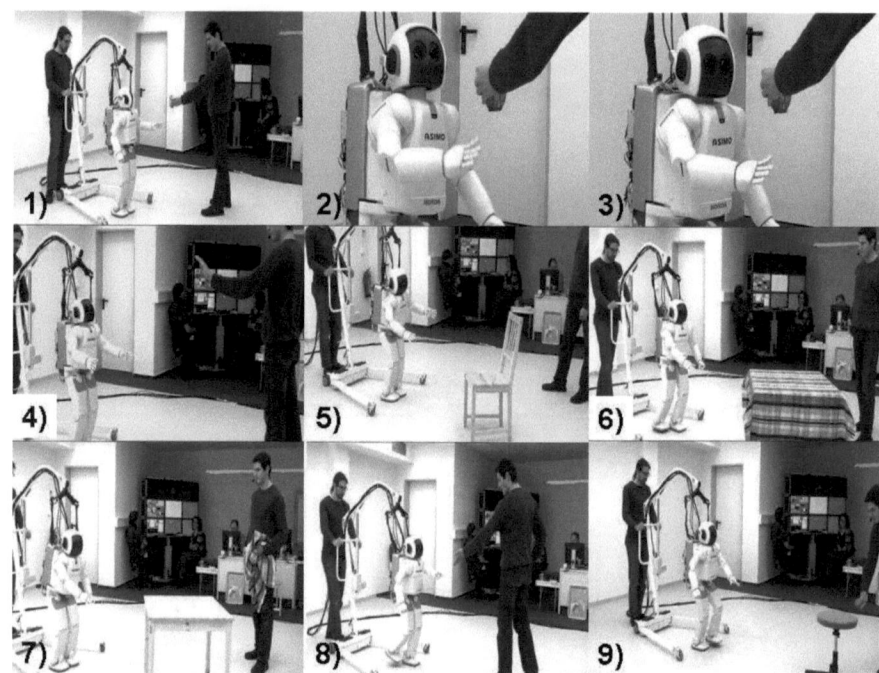

Figure 4.19: Image series from the experiment on speech learning and evaluation. 1)Fixation and pointing while learning the speech label for the left position. 2,3)Expectation evaluation: nodding as ,Yes' gesture to show the expectation match. 4)Interaction with a motion proto-object. Learning of 'still' and 'moving' labels. 5,6,7)Interaction with planar proto-objects. 5)Learning of the 'chair' label. 6)Fixation and adjustment of the interaction distance to the table and learning of the 'table' label. 7)Testing the independency from visual appearance. 8)Approaching the user and learning 'forward' label. 9)Evaluation of learnt labels on the unknown object.

4.3.4 Analysis: distribution of learning and predesign

Our long-term goal is the design of a bootstrapping system for open-ended autonomous development. For this reason we would like to carefully analyze which parts of our system can be considered necessary for bootstrapping; which parts help the designer to make further steps in incremental building; and which parts would enable the system to make further developmental steps.

In this work we consider the binding of features to a concept in form of an associative memory on the level of feature classes. Many approaches in Developmental Robotics learn models or concepts as correlations directly on the level of the features using only the statistics of the data. The problem for these bottom-up approaches is how to find the right level of generalization and

4.3 Expectation generation: beyond reactivity

how to update the models (stability-plasticity problem). As a side effect of these difficulties the research often stops at the level of correlation learning without coupling to behavior at all or using it only for simple reactive behavior.

We do not learn in a bottom-up way, instead we stabilize the learning with the help of a top-down teaching signal. As we explained in Section 4.3.1, four predesigned parts in our system contribute to the stabilization of learning at the level of a feature classifiers: predesigned feature classifiers, an evaluation mask, the way how a user generates attention, and the associative memory.

We see fixed classifiers as initial hypotheses for the system. Here our future work goes into the direction of mechanisms for autonomous generation and refining of hypotheses. The autonomous generation of hypotheses is necessary in order to scale up the system, but it does not directly contribute to the development of the behavior. We already have tested an unsupervised clustering for this purpose. In contrast, the refining of the classifier hypothesis is crucial for the grounding of the concepts and it has to be considered in conjunction with the problem of concept representation by a fixed associative memory.

Similar arguments are valid for the predesign of learning criteria as a source of attention. Since we use a well defined interface in form of expectations, the source of these expectations can easily be replaced. We have preliminary results on how to raise the expectation by monitoring repeated changes in a particular feature channel. The replacement of predesigned solution by emergent solutions would increase the number of things that can be taught to the system, without direct improvement of the learning behavior.

Next we discuss the predesign of the associative memory by fixing the association matrix instead of learning it. In case of speech learning the predesign of the association between the speech classes and non-speech classes means that the system 'knows' that the feature classes can be 'named'. In the future we will extend our system by an autonomous detection of the necessity to associate particular feature channels by monitoring whether the correlation of the features is accompanied by a reward signal. Then our approach could model the explosion of the vocabulary as observed in child development. First the language is learned slowly. This phase would correspond to bottom-up statistical learning that discovers the fact of 'naming'. In the second phase children show a rapid vocabulary increase. In our implementation this corresponds to 'naming' used for the top-down generation of a teaching signal for the speech classifier.

Crucial steps towards more complex learning behavior and a truly complete, situated system are an integration of more complex behavior for resolving expectation mismatches and an integration of rewards as signals for building an associative memory.

4.3.5 Conclusions

We presented a way how a reactive layer can be extended by an abstraction layer that generates the expectations. The expectations that are not matched by sensory input activate the mismatch resolution: a behavior that stops either if the expectation is matched (with a positive answer) or after a time-out (with a negative answer). We see this behavior as a first step towards hypothesis testing and goal-directed behavior.

The main difference of our approach compared to other architectures that integrate anticipative and reactive control is that our reactive layer can be used without any control layer

4 Incremental Building of Developing Systems

above it. Thus our system is more robust: if the higher layer does not produce an output the system does not completely break, but continues to interact with the environment. Further, our expectation generation layer also does not depend on a higher layer, e.g. a planning ability, that could be added later.

In contrast, the hybrid architectures that use Reinforcement Learning (RL), for example [21] with the DEDS formalism, are forced to always evaluate the future reward and always plan. These architectures do not switch between reactive and expectation-driven modes, they only use the reactive controller within a plan. Furthermore the RL-based approaches are forced to define only one reward function. In our architecture the reward signal is planned to control the creation of the associative memories and there is no constraint on the number of such memories. Thus with our design we create the potential to build a system that can deal with multiple competing reward signals.

The loose coupling of abstractions to the reactive behavior has several advantages compared to including a direct action representation into the abstract concept, as it is usually done in the anticipative systems with prediction of action outcome (see [12] for an overview). First, it allows for a sufficient decoupling of the dynamics of the concept learning from the dynamics of the behavior. This leads both to a stabilization and transparency of the overall behavior (see [48] for the problems due to the tight coupling). Second, it allows to link a multitude of behaviors to the same concept. Finally, it provides the possibility to use the concepts as the subject of higher mental functions (attention, communication, planning, memorization) in the sense of symbol detachment problem as discussed in [44].

In the framework of open-ended development we set a high value on task/scenario independent solutions, flexible interfaces, and the possibility of growing and scaling up. Below we summarize the design features that support the incremental building of an intelligent system:

- a generic concept of proto-objects allows for bootstrapping the system with stable, task-unspecific reactive behavior [9];

- all feature channels are handled in a similar way for easy integration of additional feature channels;

- a mask decides which feature channel generates an expectation, therefore it can be replaced by an internally generated mask later without a system redesign;

- there is no explicitly coded teaching signal, instead the mechanism of expectation generation is used.

In summary, both the coupling of mental concepts to the reactive layer and a flexible design allow for further steps in incremental building of autonomously developing systems.

4.4 Summary

In this chapter we tested on real-world experiments our general ideas about the system design formulated in Chapter 3. We built a reactive layer for general interaction with the environment and extended it by increasingly complex types of abstraction layers.

4.4 Summary

We started first with a simple type of abstraction based on a clustering of the sensorimotor space (type A:SM:R). We showed that with the help of a homeostatic control of the general rewards for learning progress and for being in interaction, this simple abstraction type together with a simple heuristic for parameter exploration can bootstrap the progress of the system from reflexive to differentiated gazing.

We focused next on the problems of learning in dynamically changing environments. In order to deal with these problems we used the abstraction type A:SE:O. We demonstrated that by using a differentiation between short-term and long-term statistics we can stably couple the exploration and online-learning with behavior switching.

We finally implemented a system that uses abstractions of type A:SE:R for generation of the expectations. These are used for learning and for generation of expectation-driven behavior. The uniform design supports the processing of multiple different feature channels (in our example: vision, speech, action). The abstraction layer is coupled to a reactive layer by a link that activates the resolution of the expectation mismatch. This architecture allows to use both reactive and expectation-driven behaviors and paves the way towards goal-driven behavior generation that can integrate planning and hypothesis testing.

4 Incremental Building of Developing Systems

5 Summary and Conclusions

The majority of applications in Developmental Robotics aim at learning of one isolated specific ability. The development stops as soon as the ability is learned and the system has to be redesigned if the robot should learn another ability. The goal of our work is to investigate the design of an initial system that can bootstrap an open-ended, task-unspecific development.

In Chapter 3 we formulated general design principles and the requirements on the bootstrapping system. The bootstrapping consists of three elements:

1. Innate behaviors that provide a general and robust interaction with the environment on a short-time scale.

2. The value system that monitors the reward acquisition on a long-time scale.

3. The abstraction system that acts on a middle-time scale. The abstraction system monitors the interaction with respect to the rewards in order to provide control alternatives to innate behaviors.

To obtain progress compared to existing approaches we used some design principles observed in the brain. As for innate behaviors, we start with an autonomous reactive system instead of basic actions that have to be controlled by higher layers, which is the conventional way. Such a design provides a higher stability of the system as well as better possibilities for observation and control of the reactive layer. Instead of reward maximization used by classical Reinforcement Learning, we use a homeostatic control that allows to work with multiple conflicting rewards. And instead of sticking to one abstraction type we use multiple abstraction types that can support the development of each other. A crucial difference of our work compared to the majority of applications is that both the innate behaviors and the reward system are not task-specific but provide a general ability to interact with the environment and to judge the quality of interaction. Further, we do not focus on the quantitative growth of the system's abilities but on the qualitative transition from reactive to expectation driven behavior.

We validated our proposed design by giving examples of possible implementations of the bootstrapping system in Chapter 4. We followed the guidelines proposed by psychologists to robotics, [55]:

- **Be physical.** Our tests were done in the real-world, not in a simulation. Although the real-world implementations require an additional effort, they prevent a researcher from making unrealistic assumptions about the system and the environment. Moreover, the hardware is indispensable in the developmental scenarios that actively use the interaction with the environment, e.g. focusing an object for learning how to recognize it (Section 4.1).

- **Be social.** Social interaction is an important part of the interaction with the environment in all of our applications. The human plays multiple roles: he provides a teaching

5 Summary and Conclusions

signal (see Section 4.1) and structures the statistics of observations so as to facilitate the learning (see Sections 4.1 and 4.3). Further, by overinterpretation of the system's behavior, a human shows regularities that can be used as new goals (see Section 4.2). Dealing with social interaction made us aware of difficulties that can appear if we apply standard methods of statistical learning to a highly dynamic environment. We developed countermeasures to stabilize the learning. We made a careful differentiation between different types of prediction errors (Section 4.2) and we designed a system with subparts that are tightly integrated but decoupled in learning (Section 4.3).

- **Be incremental.** Our aim is to build a comprehensive complex system. Such endeavor can be accomplished only in small steps, otherwise we can not handle the complexity and can not analyze the internal processes in the system. In our work we increased the complexity of the hardware from the robot head only, to the head with simulated hand gestures, to finally the whole humanoid robot ASIMO. On the software side we progressed from optimization of the parameters in an existing architecture to adding new layers and from dealing with only vision to dealing with both vision and speech.

- **Be multimodal.** Multimodality allows to observe correlations, which exist between different channels. In Section 4.3 we used vision, speech, and action-related features to create the expectation models. Using these models the system can qualitatively change the behavior from reactive to expectation-driven. Further, the expectations cross-support the learning of the classes in the distinct channels. In our particular example we investigated the learning of the speech labels but we designed the system in such a way that every channel was treated in the same way.

- **Learn a language.** In Section 4.3 we have done the first step towards learning a language. This is an important step because with the help of language a human can attract the attention of a system to regularities that may be missed otherwise. It introduces the structure in the observations that can speed up the learning on the higher abstraction layers. In our system we attached great importance to embedding language into the behavior generation. First, the behavior labels can be used as commands to a robot. Second, the speech label associated with visual features activates the undirected search for these features. This behavior can be useful for the refinement of concepts. For both cases we use the same mechanism of expectation generation and resolution of the expectation mismatch. Such uniform system design increases both the transparency of the architecture and the consistency of the behavior.

The presented work creates a good starting point for further investigations on the development of a complete system with coupled dynamics of changing needs, changing internal representations, and changing behavior, because it proposes several methods for the stabilization of the system's behavior.

First, the decomposition of the abstraction layer proposed in Section 4.3 allows learning of different structures at different time-spans. In the current experiment the system learned only at the level of feature classification. Further work can incorporate the learning on the level of the associative memory guided by observations of the reward. Also the cross-support of learning in different channels can be investigated further: the current implementation used only one improvement step where the non-speech channels teach the speech channel, whereas the steps can be repeated by letting the improved speech channel teach the non-speech channels. The top-down/bottom-up loops in the expectation generation mechanisms can account for such incremental progress in multiple channels.

The second stabilizing factor is the loose coupling of the abstractions to the behaviors over the activation of mismatch resolution. In this way we can better decouple changing internal representations and changing behaviors, compared to a direct representation of the actions in an abstraction unit. This feature allows to introduce more elaborated hypothesis testing and disambiguation. The far-future goal can be a system that integrates planning with hypothesis testing. The expectation mechanism provides a good starting point because in our architecture it is a uniform interface for goal-directed behavior, hypothesis testing and learning.

Above we suggested further research in the direction of increasingly complex control. On the other side it is important to make the system broader and increase the spectrum of behaviors by adding more rewards, both general and specific. For example, additionally to the investigated rewards for interaction, learning progress, and controllability it would be interesting to investigate the reward that measures agreement of the human with the robot's behavior or the specific rewards e.g. for touching sensation. The proposed homeostatic control was tested for the two-dimensional case and can be used as a base for investigations of the system behavior in case of higher dimensions of the reward vector.

Although the way to the implementation of the task-unspecific open-ended artificial development is still a long one, this work has shown the first steps. We proposed a design of the initial bootstrapping system that was validated by multiple implementations of the real-world online learning from interaction between the robot and its environment. Several design features inspired by the brain research - homeostatic control, parallel representation structures, loose coupling between parallel control layers - contribute to the overall stability of the proposed architecture and make it attractive for further research.

5 Summary and Conclusions

List of Used Symbols

$\vec{N}(t)$	vector of needs
$\vec{R}(t)$	vector of rewards
B^r	reactive layer
$L_i, i \in [1 \ldots N^r]$	local controllers of the reactive layer
D	competitive selection mechanism (arbiter)
F_i	fitness of the controller L_i
β_i	bias of the controller L_i
C_i	competitive advantage
$S(t)$	sensory input
$M(t)$	motor command
$W_i^r\, i \in [1 \ldots N^r]$	mapping to motor commands implemented by controller L_i
B^a	abstraction layer
$A_j, j \in [1 \ldots N^a]$	abstraction unit
$W_j^a, j \in [1 \ldots N^a]$	mapping to motor commands implemented by abstraction A_j
$E(\ldots)$	models for expectation generation (associative or predictive)
w_D, w_M, w_V	weights of the channels in saliency map
$G_i(\vec{x}, \vec{\mu}_i, \mathbf{\Sigma_i})$	Gaussian function
$\vec{\mu}_i$	the mean of the Gaussian
$\mathbf{\Sigma}_i$	the covariance matrix of the Gaussian
π_i	the weights of the gaussian mixture model (GMM)
$\widehat{\pi}_i(t)$	the short-term statistics of the GMM weights
c	index of the feature channel
$\vec{I}_c^{bu}(t_c)$	bottom-up input
$\vec{I}_c^{td}(t_c)$	top-down input
$\vec{H}_c^R(t_c)$	request
$\vec{H}_c^Y(t_c)$	match
$\vec{H}_c^N(t_c)$	mismatch
$\vec{H}_c^S(t_c)$	internal state
$\vec{\mathcal{E}}$	evaluation mask
$\mathbf{A}$	association matrix
$\vec{E}^f(t)$	expectation generated by match (confirmation)
$\vec{E}^i(t)$	expectation generated by request (expectation)
$\vec{E}^l(t)$	expectation generated by learning criteria
$\vec{E}(t)$	combined expectation

Bibliography

[1] G. Alexander, M. Crutcher, and M. DeLong. Basal ganglia-thalamocortical circuits: parallel substrates for motor, oculomotor, "prefrontal" and "limbic" functions. *Prog. Brain. Res.*, 85:119–46, 1990.

[2] R. C. Arkin. Reactive robotic systems. In M. A. Arbib, editor, *The Handbook of Brain Theory and Neural Networks*, pages 793–796. The MIT Press, 1998.

[3] C. Balkenius. Biological learning and artificial intelligence. *Lund Univiversity Cognitive Studies*, 30, 1994.

[4] T. Bergener, C. Bruckhoff, P. Dahm, H. JanSSen, F. Joublin, R. Menzner, A. Steinhage, and W. von Seelen. Complex behavior by means of dynamical systems for an anthropomorphic robot. *Neural Networks*, 12(7-8):1087–1099, October 1999.

[5] K. Berridge and M. Kringelbach. Affective neuroscience of pleasure: reward in humans and animals. *Psychopharmacology*, 199(3):457–480, August 2008.

[6] A. Billard, Y. Epars, S. Calinon, G. Cheng, and S. Schaal. Discovering Optimal Imitation Strategies. *Robotics & Autonomous Systems, Special Issue: Robot Learning from Demonstration*, 47(2-3):69–77, 2004.

[7] C. M. Bishop. *Pattern Recognition and Machine Learning (Information Science and Statistics)*. Springer, August 2006.

[8] D. Blank, D. Kumar, L. Meeden, and J. Marshall. Bringing up robot: Fundamental mechanisms for creating a self-motivating, self-organizing architecture. *Cybernetics and Systems*, 36(2), 2005.

[9] B. Bolder, M. Dunn, M. Gienger, H. Janßen, H. Sugiura, and C. Goerick. Visually guided whole body interaction. In *IEEE International Conference on Robotics and Automation (ICRA 2007)*. IEEE, 2007.

[10] V. Braitenberg. *Vehicles: Experiments with Synthetic Psychology*. MIT Press, Cambridge, Mass., 1984.

[11] H. Brandl, F. Joublin, and C. Goerick. Towards unsupervised online word clustering. In *Proceedings of International Conference on Acoustics Speech, and Signal Processing*, pages 5073–76, 2008.

[12] M. V. Butz, O. Sigaud, G. Pezzulo, and G. Baldassarre. *Anticipatory Behavior in Adaptive Learning Systems: Advances in Anticipatory Processing*. Springer LNAI 4520, 2007.

Bibliography

[13] M. W. Doniec, G. Sun, and B. Scassellati. Active learning of joint attention. In *IEEE-RAS International Conference on Humanoid Robots (Humanoids 2006), Genova, Italy*, December 2006.

[14] K. Doya. What are the computations of the cerebellum, the basal ganglia and the cerebral cortex? *Neural Networks*, 12(7-8):961–974, October 1999.

[15] K. Doya. Metalearning and neuromodulation. *Neural Networks*, 15(4):495–506, 2002.

[16] J. Eggert and H. Wersing. Approaches and challenges on the road towards a cognitive vision system. In B. Sendhoff, E. Koerner, O. Sporns, H. Ritter, and K. Doya, editors, *Creating Brain-like Intelligence 2007*. Springer Verlag, LNCS Series, 2007.

[17] M. U. Gienger, H. Janßen, and C. Goerick. Task-oriented whole body motion for humanoid robots. In *Proceedings of the IEEE-RAS International Conference on Humanoid Robots*, pages 238–244. IEEE Press, 2005. Tsukuba, Japan.

[18] C. Goerick, I. Mikhailova, H. Wersing, and S. Kirstein. Biologically motivated visual behaviors for humanoids: Learning to interact and learning in interaction. In *Proceedings of the IEEE/RSJ International Conference on Humanoid Robots (Humanois 2006), Genoa, Italy*. IEEE/RSJ, 2006.

[19] C. Goerick, H. Wersing, I. Mikhailova, and M. Dunn. Peripersonal space and object recognition for humanoids. In *Proceedings of the IEEE/RSJ International Conference on Humanoid Robots (Humanois 2005), Tsukuba, Japan*, 2005.

[20] M. Goetting, H. Wersing, J. Steil, E. Koerner, and H. Ritter. Adaptive scene dependent filters in online learning environments. In M. Verleysen, editor, *Proceedings of the European Symposium on Neural Networks*, pages 101–106. D-Side Publications, 2006.

[21] S. Hart, S. Ou, J. Sweeney, and R. Grupen. A framework for learning declarative structure. In *Robotics: Science and Systems - Workshop on Manipulation for Human Environments*. Philadelphia, Pennsylvania, August 2006.

[22] M. Haruno and M. Kawato. Heterarchical reinforcement-learning model for integration of multiple cortico-striatal loops; fMRI examination in stimulus-action-reward association learning. *Neural Networks*, 19:1242Ü–1254, 2006.

[23] J. M. Herrmann, M. Holicki, and R. Der. On Ashby's homeostat. *From animals to animats 8. Proceedings of the Seventh International Conference on Simulation of Adaptive Behavior*, pages 324–333, 2004.

[24] M. Hersch, F. Guenter, S. Calinon, and A. G. Billard. Learning dynamical system modulation for constrained reaching tasks. In *Proceedings of the 6th IEEE-RAS International Conference on Humanoid Robots, (Humanois 2006), Genoa, Italy*, pages 444–449, 2006.

[25] M. Huber and R. A. Grupen. Learning to coordinate controllers - reinforcement learning on a control basis. In *IJCAI, International joint conference on Artificial Intelligence, Nagoya, Japan*, pages 1366–1371, 1997.

Bibliography

[26] M. Huber and R. A. Grupen. A framework for the development of robot behavior. Technical report, University of Massachusetts Amherst, Dept of Computer Science, 2005.

[27] L. Itti, C. Koch, and E. Niebur. A model of saliency-based visual attention for rapid scene analysis. *IEEE Transactions on Pattern Analysis and Machine Intelligence*, 20(11):1254–1259, 1998.

[28] C. C. Kemp and A. Edsinger. What can I control?: A framework for robot self-discovery. In *Proceedings of the Sixth International Conference on Epigenetic Robotics, Paris, France*, September 2006.

[29] S. Kirstein, H. Wersing, and E. Körner. Rapid online learning of objects in a biologically motivated recognition architecture. In *27th Pattern Recognition Symposium DAGM*, pages 301–308. Springer, 2005.

[30] A. S. Klyubin, D. Polani, and C. L. Nehaniv. Empowerment: a universal agent-centric measure of control. In *Congress on Evolutionary Computation*, pages 128–135. IEEE, 2005.

[31] E. Körner and G. Matsumoto. Cortical architecture and self-referential control for brain-like processing in artificial neural systems. *Artificial life and robotics*, 2(3):170–178, 1998.

[32] A. Kulakov and G. Stojanov. Structures, inner values, hierarchies and stages: Essential for developmental robot architectures. In C. G. Prince, Y. Demiris, Y. Marom, H. Kozima, and C. Balkenius, editors, *Proceedings of the Second International Workshop on Epigenetic Robotics, Edinburgh, Scotland*, pages 63–69, 2002.

[33] M. Lungarella and L. Berthouze. Adaptivity through physical immaturity. In C. G. Prince, Y. Demiris, Y. Marom, H. Kozima, and C. Balkenius, editors, *Proceedings of the Second International Workshop on Epigenetic Robotics, Edinburgh, Scotland*, pages 79–86, 2002.

[34] M. Lungarella, G. Metta, R. Pfeifer, and G. Sandini. Developmental robotics: A survey. *Connection Science*, 15(4):151–190, 2003.

[35] M. Lungarella and O. Sporns. Mapping information flow in sensorimotor networks. *PLoS Computational Biology*, 10:1301–1312, 2006.

[36] J. Marshall, D. Blank, and L. Meeden. An emergent framework for self-motivation in developmental robotics. In *Proceedings of the third International Conference on Development and Learning (ICDL'03)*, 2004.

[37] I. Mikhailova. Saliency-based gaze direction control for active vision. Diplomarbeit, Technische Universität Darmstadt, Juni 2003.

[38] I. Mikhailova. Homeostatic control in robotics. Internal Report 05/12, Honda Research Institute Europe GmbH, D-63073 Offenbach/Main, Germany, October 2005.

[39] I. Mikhailova and C. Goerick. Conditions of activity bubble uniqueness in dynamic neural fields. *Biological Cybernetics*, 92:82–91, 2005.

Bibliography

[40] Y. Nagai, M. Asada, and K. Hosoda. A developmental approach accelerates learning of joint attention. In *Proceedings of the 2nd International Conference on Development and Learning (ICDL'02)*, pages 277–282, June 2002.

[41] P.-Y. Oudeyer and F. Kaplan. Intelligent adaptive curiosity: a source of self-development. In *Proceedings of the 4th International Workshop on Epigenetic Robotics, Genoa, Italy*, Lund University Cognitive Science Studies 117, pages 127–130, 2004.

[42] P.-Y. Oudeyer and F. Kaplan. Discovering communication. *Connection Science*, 18(2):189–206, 2006.

[43] P.-Y. Oudeyer and F. Kaplan. What is intrinsic motivation? a typology of computational approaches. *Frontiers in Neurorobotics*, 1(6), 2007.

[44] G. Pezzulo and C. Castelfranchi. The symbol detachment problem. *Cognitive Processing*, 8(2):115–131, 2007.

[45] R. Pfeifer and C. Scheier. *Understanding Intelligence*. Cambridge, MA: MIT Press., 1999.

[46] R. Platt, A. H. Fagg, and R. Grupen. Improving grasp skills using schema structured learning. In *Proceedings of the 6th International Conference on Development and Learning (ICDL'06), Bloomington, Indiana*, May 2006.

[47] C. G. Prince, N. A. Helder, and G. J. Hollich. Ongoing emergence: A core concept in epigenetic robotics. In *Proceedings of the Fifth International Workshop on Epigenetic Robotics: Modeling Cognitive Development in Robotic Systems, Nara, Japan*, July 22-24 2005.

[48] V. G. Red'ko, K. V. Anokhin, M. S. Burtsev, A. I. Manolov, O. P. Mosalov, V. A. Nepomnyashchikh, and D. V. Prokhorov. Project "animat brain": Designing the animat control system on the basis of the functional systems theory. In M. V. Butz, O. Sigaud, G. Pezzulo, and G. Baldassarre, editors, *SAB Anticipatory Behavior in Adaptive Learning Systems: From Brains to Individual and Social Behavior (ABiALS)*, pages 94–107. Springer LNAI 4520, 2007.

[49] H. Rodman. Development of inferior temporal cortex in monkey. *Cerebral Cortex*, 4(5):484–498, 1994.

[50] J. Santamaria, R. Sutton, and A. Ram. Experiments with reinforcement learning in problems with continuous state and action spaces. *Adaptive Behavior*, 6(2):163–218, 1998.

[51] T. Sawada, T.Takagi, Y.Hoshino, and M.Fujita. Learning behavior selection through interaction based on emotionally grounded symbol concept. In *Proceedings of the EEE-RAS/RSJ International Conference on Humanoid Robots (Humanoids 2004)*, November 10-12, 2004.

[52] J. Schmüdderich, V. Willert, J. Eggert, S. Rebhan, C. Goerick, G. Sagerer, and E. Körner. Detecting objects proper motion using optical flow, kinematics and depth information. *IEEE Transactions on Systems, Man, and Cybernetics*, 38(4):1139–1151, Aug 2008.

Bibliography

[53] B. Sendhoff, U. Körner, and E. Körner. On the integration of biological constraints into the evolution of artificial neural systems. In S.-Y. Lee, editor, *Seventh International Conference on Neural Information Processing – Proceedings*, pages 903–908, Taejon, Korea, 2000.

[54] S. P. Singh, A. G. Barto, and N. Chentanez. Intrinsically motivated reinforcement learning. In *18th Annual Conference on Neural Information Processing Systems (NIPS), Vancouver, B.C., Canada*, December 2004.

[55] L. Smith and M. Gasser. The development of embodied cognition: Six lessons from babies. *Artificial Life*, 11(1-2):13–30, 2005.

[56] O. Sporns and W. H. Alexander. Neuromodulation and plasticity in an autonomous robot. *Neural Networks*, 15(4):761–774, 2002.

[57] E. Thelen and E. Bates. Connectionism and dynamic systems: are they really different? *Developmental Science*, 6(4):378–391, 2003.

[58] M. Toussaint and A. J. Storkey. Probabilistic inference for solving discrete and continuous state markov decision processes. In *ICML '06: Proceedings of the 23rd international conference on Machine learning*, pages 945–952, New York, NY, USA, 2006. ACM.

[59] L. Vygodsky. *Psyhologia*. Eksmo-Press, Moscow, 2002. Collection of the fundamental works written in 1925-1934, in russian.

[60] H. Wersing, S. Kirstein, M. Goetting, H. Brandl, M. Dunn, I. Mikhailova, C. Goerick, J. Steil, H. Ritter, and E. Koerner. A biologically motivated system for unconstrained online learning of visual objects. In *Proc. ICANN*. Springer, 2006.

[61] H. Wersing and E. Körner. Learning optimized features for hierarchical models of invariant recognition. *Neural Computation*, 15(7):1559–1588, 2003.

[62] D. Wolpert and M. Kawato. Multiple paired forward and inverse models for motor control. *Neural Networks*, 11:1317–1329, 1998.

[63] H. H. Yin, S. B. Ostlund, and B. W. Balleine. Reward-guided learning beyond dopamine in the nucleus accumbens: the integrative functions of cortico-basal ganglia networks. *European Journal of Neuroscience*, in press.

[64] E. C. Zeeman and M. L. Zeeman. From local to global behavior in competitive Lotka-Volterra systems. *Trans. Amer. Math. Soc.*, 355:713–734, 2003.

[65] L. Zhang. Autonomes Lernen kontextabhängiger Handstellungen am Beispiel des Zeigens auf und des Anforderns von Objekten. Diplomarbeit, Universität Karlsruhe (TH), Juni 2006.

[66] Y. Zhang and J. Weng. Task transfer by a developmental robot. *IEEE Transaction on Evolutionary Computation*, 11(2):226–248, April 2007.

Die VDM Verlagsservicegesellschaft sucht für wissenschaftliche Verlage abgeschlossene und herausragende

Dissertationen, Habilitationen, Diplomarbeiten, Master Theses, Magisterarbeiten usw.

für die kostenlose Publikation als Fachbuch.

Sie verfügen über eine Arbeit, die hohen inhaltlichen und formalen Ansprüchen genügt, und haben Interesse an einer honorarvergüteten Publikation?

Dann senden Sie bitte erste Informationen über sich und Ihre Arbeit per Email an *info@vdm-vsg.de*.

Sie erhalten kurzfristig unser Feedback!

VDM Verlagsservicegesellschaft mbH
Dudweiler Landstr. 99   Telefon +49 681 3720 174
D - 66123 Saarbrücken   Fax   +49 681 3720 1749

www.vdm-vsg.de

Die VDM Verlagsservicegesellschaft mbH vertritt

Printed by Books on Demand GmbH, Norderstedt / Germany